BRIGHT
VALLEY
OF LOVE

BRIGHT VALLEY OF LOVE

Edna Hong

AUGSBURG Publishing House
Minneapolis, Minnesota

This book is dedicated to the memory
of our godchild, Dorothee Funke,
whose father, Pastor Alex Funke,
is the present director
of the Bodelschwingh institutions,
including Bethel.

CONTENTS

To love forth love is to build up. But to love forth love means precisely to presuppose that it is present at the base.

—SØREN KIERKEGAARD

PROLOG

This is a true-to-life story. Gunther was a real live boy and now is a real live man. I met him, talked with him, and walked with him in June of 1974.

This is a true-to-place story. Bethel is a real city in a real valley in Germany. In fact, I found it so true a place that I decided it must be one of the most gospel-true places in the world! In no other place have I found love lived so true-to-the-gospel, twenty-four hours a day and every day of the week, as in Bethel.

This is a true-to-the-larger-facts story. It is as faithful to Gunther's life, to the painful life of the epileptics, to the story of Bethel, and to the history of the times as I could make it without writing a dry and full-of-too-many-facts history book or a medical text book. Of course I had to imagine all the "he saids" and "she saids," for there were no tape recorders then!

A very wise woman—Simone Weil was her name—once wrote that *imagined* evil is fascinating and inviting, while *real* evil is deadening and repellent. But *imagined* good is dull and uninteresting, while *real* good is fascinating and inviting. Simone Weil is so right, so right! I could never have imagined good as exciting and inviting as I found it *for real* in Bethel. If I had used every ounce of my imagination, I could never have dreamed up such exciting and interesting characters as Pastor Fritz von Bodelschwingh and his wife Frau Julia. Or that gleeful trumpeter of God, Pastor Johannes Kuhlo! Indeed, I have to confess that the Gunther I imagined into the story before I ever went to Bethel was not nearly as fascinating as the *real* Gunther I finally met. I hope you will find the real Gunther I tried to place between these covers just as fascinating.

NOTHING
BUT A NOTHING

In the world of his mother's womb, the fluid of life which trickled into him through his umbilical cord was weak and starved. The world into which he was born one day in the year 1914 nourished him no better. Perhaps even worse. For it was the worst of times, and his mother was not the best of mothers. And his father went off to World War I, which the whole world lost, although some countries thought that they had won it. For the baby boy Gunther, who was born in Germany—the country that lost the war most hurtfully—the sum of all these things was a lifetime as a cripple.

"No good for anything," said his grandmother coldly when the war was all over and his father rescued him from the woman who was not the best of mothers and brought him to her own house in a great gray dingy city west of the Rhine, north of the Ruhr, and south of the Lippe rivers.

The grandmother had swept and scrubbed floors and rubbed clothes on a washboard practically every day she could remember of her life, and she believed that only people who did something useful like that had any right whatsoever to live in the world. Or people who were rich enough not to have to be useful.

Although the grandmother's own spine was crooked and curved from everlastingly bending over a washboard doing laundry for the better folk, the long bones of her legs and the short bones of her feet could do what her will commanded them to do. Even though her shoulders were hunched as if all her life she had crept through low doorways, the long bones of her arms and the short bones of her hands could be moved by her muscles when the message came over the nerves from her brain to clutch, to lift, to hold, to let go. Even when she was weary-to-death from a long day's work, her legs and her feet would take her to the woods and her arms and hands would collect deadwood in a little handcart. Even though her hands trembled, she could peel the potatoes or the turnips that were to be their supper.

But this grandchild of hers who ought to be gathering the deadwood, emptying the slop pail in the gutter below, and carrying out the ashes for her—this brat was not worth one dry twig or a bucket of potato peelings and rotten cabbage leaves! He was human junk, that's what he was, that's all he was. Deformed from head to foot. Leg bones and ankle bones. Arm bones, wrist bones, and finger bones Skull bones and jaw bones. Back bones and pelvic bones—all of them deformed!

Soft and spongy baby bones, starved of calcium and sunshine—terribly starved!—had stayed soft and spongy too long and too late. And now all the bone-warps and bone-faults had hardened once and for all. Even the knees, elbows, wrists, and ankles had stiffened and hardened. The hands looked as if they had been stuck on his arms by a blind man wearing boxing gloves. The feet seemed to have been screwed on by someone who did not make the last quarter-turn, for they did not point true and straight ahead. Lame from head to foot he was, and very likely lame-brained, too, for the sounds that came out of his throat were more babbling than speaking. The large head would roll, the thin, twisted body would strain and struggle just to say something that sounded like, "Ah-h wanna! Ah-h wanna!"

And that, it seemed, was what this brat of a grandchild would be all his misborn days—a piece of human junk that croaked, "Ah-h wanna! Ah-h wanna!"

Because the grandmother was ashamed of him and feared the tittletattlers in the neighborhood, she kept him behind the closed door of her one and only bedroom. When she came home one day and found that he had rolled himself off his cot in the back corner and pulled himself into the kitchen, she was both alarmed and angry. Ignoring his panting, gurgling cries of victory, she carried him back and dropped him roughly on his cot. When he protested and cried, "Ah-h wanna! Ah-h wanna!" she flew into a rage. "Ain't it enough that I gotta feed you and wash you? Ain't it enough that you choke on every spoon of soup I put in your mouth? Are you gonna start rammin' round now and cause me more trouble yet?"

After that she locked the bedroom door as well as the door that led from the tiny kitchen to the gloomy back stairway. To make sure that he would be quiet while she was gone, she gave him a tablesoon of Soothing Syrup, an old remedy the advertising claimed would "allay all pain, cure wind colic, and relieve diarrhea." Not that he cried very much—or loudly—if and when he did. Since his crying had always been ignored in the past, he had given up crying as an infant means of telling his needs. Most of the time he slept fitfully—or sat propped up on a pillow in a kind of dull suffering. The daily double-dose of Soothing Syrup was merely to make sure that he did not disturb the neighbors above or below or across the narrow courtyard.

For a whole year, the year he was six, the back room in his grandmother's tiny flat was his world. Since in many respects it was a better world than the cheap single room in which he had lived the other five years of his life, he was not especially miserable or sad. If someone has never seen a cherry tree, never picked and tasted a fat, plump red cherry, has never heard that there is such a thing as a cherry tree— well, he simply does not miss cherries or long for cherries or cry because he does not have any cherries. If he is hungry, he cries for the thin watery turnip soup and black bread that is his customary food. If he has to wait a long time for his supper, he lies and daydreams about a hot boiled potato, white, mealy, and melting in the mouth. His mouth waters and maybe a little spittle-water trickles out of the corner of his mouth and runs off the cliff of his chin. All that for a boiled potato with no butter, no cream sauce, no rich meat gravy—just a plain boiled potato.

A yearling calf that has never left the barn in which it was born is not especially miserable or sad with its life in a dimly lit stable—that is, if in the pattern of its day it is watered and fed regularly and given clean straw to lie upon. To the grandmother's credit, it must be said that she dutifully spoon-fed the little cripple in the back room, dutifully lifted him on the potty-chair every morning and evening. She smacked his wet bottom if he had not been able to wait, but then dutifully proceeded to change the sheet. After all, a woman who prided herself that her floors were so clean a person could eat off them could do no less. The animal in the little cripple in the back room appreciated every bit of it.

In fact, the boy even seemed to appreciate the grandmother's daily dose of irritable or bitter grumbling. It, too, became a pattern, the only voice in the voicelessness of his world.

"You're a nothing! You're nothing but a nothing!" she sometimes told him.

When the boy's solemn dark eyes perked up and registered his appreciation at being personally addressed—for nobody ever talked to him—she laughed maliciously.

"You're such a nothing you don't even know what a nothing is."

Now and then, however, the boy's animal contentment with a routine that took care of his simplest physical needs was strangely disturbed. It was as if his back-room world received a telegram from another world. It was quite another message than the ones he got through the window from the ringing of church bells and the clatter of horses' hoofs and cart wheels on rough cobblestones (remember, this was before streets whooshed, screeched, roared, and honked). It was as if someone or something was trying to inform him of something he ought to know. As if a presence was trying to push into a great absence. Something secret, wonderful, and too big to grasp. At such times his patterned contentment was punctured with joy or grief—or both at once.

One such message came from the red checkered tablecloth the woman on the second floor hung on a clothes line strung from her window. Once a week the red checkered tablecloth floated out there before his eyes. Every Monday morning, rain or shine, winter and summer. Whether it sagged and dripped with rain or fluttered and snapped in the breeze, the red checkered tablecloth filled him with a strange joy. Something far different and much more than the pleasure of the first spoon of warm lentil soup trickling down his throat on a day when he could see his own breath in the back room. Something far different and much more than the feel of a dry bed after lying in cold dampness

17

half the day. It was a telegram from another world of something unknown. Yet it was not a banner of pure joy, for it seemed to be telling him also of something missing. Not something lost, but of something he had never had.

Then there was the summer day when the grandmother left the window open, and he heard the woman who hung out the red checkered tablecloth call to a child in the courtyard below.

"Bettina, Liebchen, I forgot to tell you something—."

"What, Mommy?" piped a little voice below.

"I love you to pieces!"

It was the meaning in the tone of the mother's voice and the delicious trill of laughter from below that communicated—not joy—but a sudden and terrible grief—to the cripple in the back room. He rolled off the cot to the floor, beat the useless clubs of his feet and hands on the floor. His whole body shook with a feeling neither his mind nor his mouth could articulate. That day he messed both himself and the floor so clean a person could eat off it. When his grandmother came home from work, she scolded him savagely, and there was no supper.

"I tell you, I won't put up with that brat much longer," she said to her son when he returned from his hopeless search for a job in the cities of the Ruhr.

"I've found myself a woman," he told her glumly. "Maybe when we get married she'll take him."

"You can find a wife, but you can't find a job," sneered the grandmother.

But the new wife put her foot down and would have nothing to do with a crippled stepson, and that was that.

And the grandmother put her foot down one day when in her hurry to go to the green grocer before the shop closed she left both the door to the back room and the kitchen unlocked. This time the neighborhood boys, who had often sneaked up the back steps in their curiosity to see the kid kept in the back room, got in. They tiptoed across the kitchen and opened the door.

"Jeez!" they cried in unison.

"What a mug!" said one.

"He's a loony!" said the other.

"He ain't human!" said the third.

The grandmother, who had come up the stairs behind them, heard every word. They fled before her screams of rage, dodged her blows.

"I ain't gonna put up with it anymore!" she said to her son when he paid his guilty visit that night. "He's gotta go to an institution. You gotta take him to that place called Bethel."

"Bethel is just for people with the falling sickness," he said.

"They take cripples and idiots, too, I hear."

The boy did not understand that his familiar patterned world was about to collapse until the two of them, the grandmother and the father, carried him out of the back room and began to thrust his limbs into unfamiliar clothes, Shamefacedly avoiding his eyes, the father told him that he was going away. He and the grandmother would go with him to the place. They would not stay with him. They would come back. He would not come back. He was going to stay there in that place.

The boy understood. That was his moment of truth. In that moment he understood not only the pain and fear of this present happening, but the pain and shame of the past. He was a cast-off. He had always been a cast-off. But to be cast off into a fearful unknown—! No, not that!

With a quick, animal-like jerk, he flung himself from his father's arms to the floor. Rolling over on his stomach, he lifted himself on his twisted hands and feet. Like an animal at bay he faced them. In short panting sounds, as clear as ever he had spoken, he cried: "Ah-h don' wanna! Ah-h don' wanna!"

THE HOUSE
CALLED PATMOS

"Ah, so here we have another helpless little mite," said Pastor Wolf, taking the burden of boy from the shamefaced father's arms. "And what is your name?" he asked, looking searchingly into the boy's somber eyes.

Silence. The same dull silence that had lasted the long train ride to Bielefeld and the long walk in the drizzling rain to the Bethel Reception Center. Even when the grandmother had lagged half a length behind and her umbrella had dripped right into his face, the boy had made no sound.

"His name is Gunther," said the father.

"Does Gunther talk?"

"Not much," the grandmother answered curtly.

"Do *you* talk to Gunther?"

"What's there to say—to the likes of him?" snapped the grandmother.

The pastor's arms instinctively held the boy closer to him. "Everything!" he said. "The more these poor little ones suffer, the more we have to say to them."

"Gunther," he said directly to the boy, "we are going to send you to live with the boys and girls in the house called Patmos. Patmos is named after the Greek island where Christ's beloved John had a vision and a revelation. I think, my son, that in Patmos your little soul will also have a vision and a revelation."

The house called Patmos was farther up the snug valley between the wooded Teutoburg hills, and Pastor Wolf asked a boy passing on the street to show them the way. The boy, however, disappeared into the bakery, from which floated fragrances that would tempt even a man with a stainless-steel will.

For an hour the old woman and the man wandered up steep streets and down, too shy to ask the way again. Finally when they ended up in a cemetery on a high hill with rows and rows of neat white crosses, the grandmother stopped two girls wandering hand in hand among the graves. When they turned their faces to her—one sightless and vacant and the other birthmarked a corrugated purplish red, the question on her lips stuttered to a stop. The sunken eyes in the grotesque mask surveyed her quietly. The thick lips moved in song:

> O happy they in God who rest,
> No more by fear and doubt oppressed;
> Living or dying, they are blest!

Both girls broke into a ringing chorus of Alleluias that followed the stumbling, fleeing three down the steep path to the street below.

A man with a bountiful beard and carrying a trumpet came clattering down the street in wooden clogs.

"Do you suppose he's looney, too?" the grandmother whispered. Not being sure, she let her son ask, "Please, sir, can you tell us the way to Patmos?"

"Patmos!" chuckled the man, his eyes twinkling and dancing. "So you want to go to Patmos. How very, very remarkable that you are going the same place I am going! Follow me."

Placing himself before them like a general before his troops, he put his trumpet to his lips and began to blow. And the song he blew was an old folksong, "All the birds are here again."

Looking back over his shoulder and seeing them still standing uncertainly in the same place, he blew another tune: "O, come, little children. O come, one and all."

"He's looney, too! They're all looney here!" muttered the grandmother.

"Maybe so and maybe not," answered the father. "Maybe they're sane and we're the looney ones."

Whereupon he shifted his hold on the boy, who had squirmed from a dull and listless prone position to a sitting-up position—almost as if he had been sleeping and the trumpet blowing had waked him up. His body leaned and swayed toward the bearded trumpeter, who waved his trumpet merrily, faced about again and resumed the march to Patmos. Like the veteran soldier that he was, the father fell in step behind the jolly general, and the utterly weary, utterly confused old grandmother trotted along—two paces behind now. She was sure that the two smiling deaconesses they met, the two laughing young men pushing two patients in wheelchairs—the patients grinning from ear to ear— were all laughing at the three of them. Everybody in this looney place was laughing at them!

It was a somewhat long and crooked way, and by the time they arrived at Patmos the clear notes of the trumpet playing its merry tune had already announced their coming. A little crowd awaited them. Laughing, shouting, and waving, they crawled, limped, tottered, and staggered toward them, stretching out their hands.

"Kuhlo! Kuhlo!" they cried. "Pastor Kuhlo is coming!"

He took each hand, one by one. "Monika, my little thrush! Gisela, my skylark! Heinz, my red-headed woodpecker! See, my little birds, I have brought you another little warbler to sing praises with you. I haven't asked him his name yet—."

"His name is Gunther," said the grandmother quickly, to cover up the boy's silence. After one swift horrified look at the children, her eyes darted here and there and everywhere but to those dismaying faces so robbed of all the human graces. Their hands reached out to touch some part of him, and their mouths formed his name, repeated it until it became a chorus. The boy looked down in wonder, half fearful that it was all true, half fearful that perhaps it all was a dream.

A deaconess in a long black dress and crisp white cap, its big bow tied under her chin, pushed her way gently through the crowd of children, leading a blind boy.

"O, Willi, my little Willi, here is a new friend for you," said Pastor Kuhlo. "Gunther, this is Willi. He was born without eyes, but God gave his heart eyes that see far better than yours or mine."

The boy perched in his father's arms looked into the turned-up face with deep sockets where eyes should be. Slowly he dropped his right arm he had arched around his father's neck and touched the groping hand. As if through thick mittens his rigid hand felt the blind boy's fingers touch the stiff pegs that were his own.

"Sister Mathilde, my bonny magpie," said Pastor Kuhlo, "We have brought you another nestling for your nest. Gunther, this is your Tante Mathilde."

"Come, my son," he said to the father. "Cast all your burdens upon him who said 'Suffer the little children to come unto me.' Sister Mathilde's arms are his arms."

Pastor Kuhlo's eyes rested on the old grandmother and the father, whose misery was growing by the minute.

"You see," he said softly, "Bethel is no walled city. Our only walls are the green walls of our mountain valley. Here is no huge institution. We are simply and solely the arms of Christ. You need have no fear to leave Gunther here."

Abruptly, almost savagely, the father deposited the boy in the deaconess's waiting arms. "Not fear, Pastor," he blurted, "Guilt!" Without another word, not even a good-bye, he turned on his heel and hurried away, the old woman trotting three paces behind.

"They all feel that way when they leave them," sighed the deaconess. "So terribly, terribly guilty!"

"I hope they know where forgiveness is to be found," said Pastor Kuhlo. Putting his trumpet to his lips he blew Luther's words to Psalm 130 to the two dark figures hurrying out of the valley. "Out of the depths I cry to thee..."

From the opposite wooded hill the notes were echoed: "I cry to thee...."

"There are many more little birds inside, Gunther," said Pastor Kuhlo as the little procession followed the path around the flower beds to the House Patmos. "But their wings are broken, and they cannot fly. I am going in to see them and play them praise songs."

Like someone who comes suddenly from a dark room to a brightly lighted room and at first is unable to see clearly, in fact, almost seems to prefer the darkness, so Gunther's mind groped back to his dark world, clung to the dark figures he last saw hurrying, almost running, down the road out of the valley. But the clutching finger of the blind Willi held back his tears, held him in this bright new room.

"You my friend," said Willi through the bars of the clean white bed in which Sister Mathilde gently laid Gunther after she bathed him in a huge bathtub and dressed him in a white nightshirt.

"Gunther my friend," Willi told Sister Anna when she came to call him to supper. "I stay with my friend."

"But you eat in the big dining room, Willi," said Sister Anna. "You can eat by yourself. Gunther will eat in the little dining room. He needs to be helped."

"Goodbye, Gunther, I come back."

The boy in the bed did not take his eyes from the sightless face pressed against the bars of his bed. But he said nothing.

"Gunther no can talk," said Willi, walking away sadly. "I no can see. Gunther no can talk."

By the time Willi reached the door, his pool of cheerfulness was brimming over again. "Gunther, you my friend," he called. "I talk for you. You see for me."

The boy suddenly felt lonely when Willi had gone—but not desolate. By this time he already had begun to sense that the white cap the deaconesses wore was a message. The wide white bow under the chin was a banner of bright hope, like the red checkered tablecloth. And to his utter joy and amazement the red checkered tablecloth suddenly appeared in his brand-new life. His eyes spotted it immediately when Sister Mathilde carried him into the little dining room where the completely helpless children were fed. As the good Sister tied him in his chair she no doubt thought that the sudden brightening in this new child's joyless face was due to the sight of chocolate pudding. But the boy had never in his life eaten chocolate pudding. How could he know that the mushy dark brown stuff tasted so good, so good? But the red checkered tablecloth was an old friend—only he could not understand how it possibly could have followed him and gotten on this table!

The return of the red checkered tablecloth, or more properly its secret message that some glad something he had never had was now to be his, carried him through a first experience that was to become as familiar to him as wheelchairs and the helmets that epileptic patients with severe epilepsy wear to protect their heads when they fall.

Rosemarie, a little girl with a flopping head that rolled from side to side, was being fed by Sister Elizabeth. Suddenly Rosemarie made a queer sound and slumped to the right. Her right arm hit the bowl of lentil soup and knocked it across the table, spilling it all over Gunther and Sister Mathilde. Her head jerked back, her jaws clenched. As suddenly as she had gone limp, her body became stiff as a board. Slowly, jerkily, it relaxed again. With a sobbing moan she opened her eyes and looked fearfully around.

To Gunther the squares of the red tablecloth seemed to grow livid, then murky and menacing. A shiver ran through the boy's body from head to foot. Suddenly he was in Sister Mathilde's lap and she was rocking him with her swaying body, just as Rosemarie was being held and rocked by Sister Elizabeth across the table. The two deaconesses began to sing in a crooning voice that made them more than social workers, more than nurses, in fact, made them more mothers than are some mothers.

> O Jesu so meek, O Jesu so kind,
> Thou hast fulfilled thy Father's mind;
> Hast come from heaven down to earth
> In human flesh through human birth.
> O Jesu so meek, O Jesu so kind!
>
> O Jesu so good, O Jesu so meek,
> To do thy will is all we seek;
> For all we are or have is thine;
> Do thou our hearts to thee incline.
> O Jesu so good, O Jesu so meek!

The squares of the tablecloth grew bright and vivid again. Then slowly faded. So deeply did the boy sleep that he did not feel himself carried back to his bed, did not hear Willi's whispered "Goodnight, Gunther, my friend!"

LOVE IS THE BEST ANTIDOTE

The next day was Doctor Blümcke's day to visit Patmos, and of course he checked the newcomer to the house. He peered into the boy's mouth and noted the malformed lower jaw. His tenderly probing hands moved over the crooked spine, the deformed pelvis, the pigeon breast, the twisted limbs, the hands bent like a hoe, the warped feet.

"Gunther, my son," he said, and he could not keep the sadness from his voice. "I wish I had seen you when you were two. But we will see what sunshine and milk can do. We'll carry your bed out under the trees. Not too much strong August sun at first, my boy. You look as gray as the gray bugs that live in root cellars and under planks and stones. But as much milk as can be spared—milk from the American cows."

Dr. Blümcke leaned close and spoke slowly, clearly, and very directly to the alert eyes. "Has anyone told you yet of the American cows, Gunther? Just two months ago they came. Twenty-seven beautiful American cows, a big bossy bull, and a week-old calf that had a free ocean ride. I'm sure it wasn't on the original bill of lading. They were sent by Sunday school children in Chicago, church women in Detroit, and by many other Christians in America. Pastor Fritz told us about their coming way last Christmas Eve. Along about Easter we began to think that they would never come. But finally they did. By ship from New York to Bremen. By train to Bielefeld. And what a parade we had through the valley! You should have been here, Gunther! Everybody in Bethel who could walk was in it, and everybody else was at the windows. There was music, Gunther! Pastor Kuhlo and his brass band. The mouth organ orchestra. Plus flags and banners and flowers. The children had made wreaths of flowers for the cows' necks. A crown of oak leaves for His Majesty, King Americanus the Bull. And the little week-old Princess rode in a cart with long ropes of daisies twined through the spokes. We paraded, all of us—people, cows, bull, and Princess Calf. All the way from the portals of Bethel to the farm Quellenhof. And there they are today—producing milk to make you as strong and well as—as—."

The sadness returned to the doctor's eyes. "As strong as it is in our poor human power to make your poor innocent insulted body," he said, more to himself than to the boy. "I wish I had seen you when you were two!"

Before Dr. Blümcke left, he told Sister Mathilde that it was the worst case of rickets he had seen in his whole medical practice.

"Do you think it has affected his brain?" asked the deaconess. "He has not said a word since he came."

"There's a bright quivering mobility in his eyes that usually is a sign of intelligence."

"But there wasn't yesterday. In fact, he seemed rather dull and—."

"Doped, I'll bet! Oh, not deliberately. But some of the concoctions old grannies give children are narcotic drugs. The poor tired old souls think they are spooning a soothing syrup into the child, but they really are making little drug addicts of them. Well, we'll see what sunshine and milk can do. And the special brand of medicine you Sisters dole out so superabundantly."

The doctor turned to go. Genuinely alarmed, Sister Mathilde put her hand on his arm. "Dr. Blümcke, are you accusing us of—?"

"Accusing you of love, Sister Mathilde. Love! Not a narcotic, a stimulant! The best antidote to a bad beginning I know. Dose the newcomer in sunshine, milk, and love."

When Sisters Mathilde and Elizabeth came to follow the doctor's orders and take Gunther outside, they found him peering shyly through the bars of the bed at the boy in the next bed.

"So you are making friends already," laughed Sister Mathilde. "Gunther, this is Kurt. He came to us just last week. How would you two like to go up to the Beech Forest? Upsadaisy, and away we go!"

Strong arms lifted him up, and he rode up the hill in them with Sister Mathilde's crisp white chin bow pleasantly tickling his cheek. Blind Willi latched on to her apron at the door.

"I come, too," he announced. "Gunther no can talk. I talk for Gunther. I talk to Kurt for Gunther."

Willi sat between them on the blanket under the towering old beech trees, unable to see the patches of amber light that shifted on Gunther's pale arms and legs and flecked Kurt's ashen face. But the twittering of the countless children lying on cots or in hammocks slung between the trees he could and did hear.

"Listen!" he shouted in delight. "Like birds! 'All the birds are here again!' "

For the rest of the morning Willi tried to teach his two new friends the song about the birds. Kurt dozed and slept between weak attempts to show that he had learned some of the words. Gunther was so busily alive to all his five senses and receiving their exciting messages that he ignored his teacher. Real birds sang in the treetops. Children called to each other. Grownups, healthy and sick alike, took shortcuts through the woods from one side of the wooded hill to the other. And the sunlight filtered through the tops of the trees and speckled some of the leaves green-gold, and the green leaves danced with the green-gold leaves.

When Willi finally lamented his silence and said mournfully, "Gunther, you no sing! You no my friend?" Gunther rolled over and laid his head in Willi's lap. Almost as if to close his senses to all other messages, he shut his eyes, content to feel only the gentle stroking of Willi's hand. When the Sisters came to fetch the three for dinner, they were all sound asleep.

Inspired by the doctor's story about the American cows, the Sisters of Patmos organized an afternoon excursion to Quellenhof, the farm at the end of the valley where the cows were pastured. The children who could walk pulled the children who could not in carts cushioned with freshly cut grass. The farm was not far, not really, but to the Patmos children it was an enchanted far country. Quellenhof was on the edge of a forest that went on and on and on and did not just stop on the other side of the hill. The Quellenhof pastures were great fields—not just little gardens and lawns. The Quellenhof stables were big enough to hold a whole herd of cows. And the Quellenhof house was a real farm house, timbered and very solid.

They made a game of counting the cows in the pasture, and each child arrived at a different number.

"Twenty-seven cows, one bull, and one calf a week old,"

said Manfred authoritatively, not bothering to count and relying on his amazing memory. For Manfred could remember numbers, figures and isolated facts, but he could not weave his numbers and figures and isolated facts together to make any kind of sense.

"Forty-eleven cows," said Otto, counting laboriously on his fingers. "And one calf," relying on that beautifully vivid memory.

But the house father led out five calves, one just two weeks old. Manfred was so insulted to be wrong that he went behind a squat oak tree and sucked his thumb—that is, until a burst of laughter drew him back. Leni had discovered that the new calf looked like the Tante Sisters— all black, with a white cap and a bow under its chin.

It was the new black and white calf that drew forth the first laugh from Gunther. Who knows—perhaps it was the very first in his life! Sister Mathilde made a point of introducing him to the calf and the calf to him. Gunther raised his hand in a kind of instinctive salute, and the calf quickly saw a similarity between its mother's udder and this clenched bent hand with the down-tilted fingers. Grabbing a finger between its rough wet tongue and the roof of its mouth, it began to suck vigorously. When no warm milk came forth, the calf shook the hand impatiently and let go in disgust.

No one was more surprised than Gunther himself at the puffs of sound that exploded from his throat. And no one was more delighted than Sister Mathilde, who placed her hand on the calf's head in a kind of benediction and breathed a silent "Thank you" to God for the silly calf that did not know the difference between a deformed hand and its mother's udder.

"Today is Sunday!" Willi announced through the bars of Gunther's bed the next morning.

"Today is Sunday!" sang Leni in the hallway on her way to breakfast.

Until he came to the Valley of Bethel, time for Gunther had been a fog that stayed on and on and never lifted. No red-letter days. Sunday was no different from Monday. The half gloom of one day simply slipped through the gloom of night into the half-gloom of another day. Time merely went on from nothing to nothing. No periods, no commas, no question marks, no exclamation marks. No looking back to a once-upon-a-happy yesterday. Or ahead to a burnished copper tomorrow. Nothing to remember, nothing to look forward to—except perhaps the next bowl of gray potato soup.

It was his third day at Bethel. There had been a profusion and confusion of sensations. Some fearful ones, such as the strange cries that rang through Patmos when a child had an epileptic attack. Kurt, who lay in the bed next to him, had already cried out like that twice this morning.

But mostly the sensations were glad ones, trumpeting awake all that dully slept in him. Mouths that spoke his name again and again. "Gunther! You have a name. Your name is Gunther!" Eyes that looked directly and deeply into his own eyes. "We see you, Gunther, and we love what we see." And one who had no eyes to see touched him and said, "Gunther, you my friend." And the rough wet tongue of a baby calf had tickled the strange sounds of laughter from his throat.—But so far all these were simply bright new pictures in the flow of time.

Today, however, was Sunday, so they told him. Before this Sunday was over a most beautiful thing happened to Gunther. Time stopped flowing on endlessly. Time went into orbit around a light and a brightness that somehow explained all the bright pictures that had suddenly bobbed up in his life. All the bright pictures went into orbit, too. For Gunther, time found a center on that Sunday. The misshapen little planet that was Gunther began orbiting around that center.

To be sure, Gunther did not launch into orbit with a spectacular bang and a burst of light. His first consciousness of any center at all was more like the sound of the muffled scratch of a match behind a closed door and a faint glimmer of light under that door. At first he sensed it without understanding it. He sensed it first in the open-air church service in the Beech Forest that August Sunday.

The Patmos Sisters were there early with those of their children who were strong enough to be brought to the open-air church. Gunther half sat, half lay on a cot and watched the churchgoers streaming toward this place as if it were the center of the whole world. They came walking, limping, shuffling. They came in rolling chairs, in carts, on stretchers. The sick and the well, the abled and the disabled—all came together here. Scores and scores of deaconesses and deacons. House fathers with their families of men and boys faulted in mind or body or both. House mothers with their families of women and girls in like condition. Worker fathers and mothers with strong and healthy children. Disabled soldiers with empty sleeves or an empty trouser leg, neatly folded and pinned up.

Gunther gazed in wonder. His wonder shot up like an elevator when he heard the thousand or more people begin to sing. The bearded Kuhlo leading the brass and voice choirs he recognized, and his heart gave a leap. The hymn—not yet, of course. Or the significance of the words for himself and all the afflicted in body and soul who were singing it.

> Look upon us, blessed Lord,
> Take our wandering thoughts and guide us.
> We have come to hear thy word,
> With thy teaching now provide us,
> That, from earth's distractions turning,
> We thy message may be learning.

For thy Spirit's radiance bright
We, assembled here, are hoping,
If thou shouldst withhold the light,
In the dark our souls were groping.
In each word and thought direct us.
Thou, thou only, canst correct us.

Brightness of the Father's face,
Light of Light, from God proceeding,
Make us ready in this place,
Ear and heart await thy leading.
Fill with life and inspiration
Every prayer and meditation.

It was the great tide of sound gathering from all those people and converging on his ears that made its impact that first Sunday in his life, the first real Sunday in his life. Suddenly he felt an urge to know what they were singing, to know why they were singing—and to sing what they were singing—and for the same reason. He caught Sister Mathilde's eye. As her lips formed the words "Light of Light, from God proceeding" they also formed a smile that was all for him. The faintest flicker of a smile trembled for a moment on his lips.

"Uncle Pastor is coming soon! Uncle Pastor is coming soon!" chanted Leni on the way to her after dinner rest.

"Pastor Fritz is coming to tell us stories. Pastor Fritz my friend," announced Willi through the bars of Gunther's bed when he awoke from his nap.

"Uncle Pastor" or Pastor Fritz was none other than Ernst Friedrich Franz von Bodelschwingh, director of this great colony of the sick that extended even beyond the valley of Bethel. Those who loved him, and that was practically everybody, called him simply Pastor Fritz.

But the children in Patmos called him Uncle Pastor.

When they heard his step on the stairway on Sunday afternoon, those who could walk came running. Those who could not leave their beds cried his name. Those who could not cry his name feebly clapped their hands. Those who could not even do that clapped with their eyes, and so keen was the ear in that man's heart that he heard the clapping of the weakest of them the best of all.

The room was full of Patmos children, and Pastor Fritz was sitting in the center of them holding Willi on his lap when Sister Mathilde came in carrying Gunther. She slipped quietly into a chair in the outer circle.

A marvellously shiny bald head and shining eyes—Gunther was not sure which shone more! The shining eyes embraced the room full of children, and each child felt personally embraced.

"Jesus our Friend told so many stories. Which one do you want to hear today?"

"The Robber Story!"

"You mean the story of the man who was going down from Jerusalem to—to—oh, dear me, I forgot! Where was he going?"

"To Jericho!" they shouted.

"Ah, yes, to Jericho! And he fell among—"

"Robbers! And the robbers beat him up."

"Children, you know the story so well that I think we must play-act it. If I will be the man going to Jericho, who will be the robbers? The priest? The Good Samaritans? The innkeeper?"

A cast was somehow chosen in the tumult, and the play began. Pastor Fritz hippety-hopped onto the stage riding a chair, his hands on the back. The robbers rushed out, hands clenched in fists. But they stopped abruptly as if they were playing "Statues" instead of "The Good Samaritan."

"Come, robbers! Beat me up!" prompted the traveller.

"Uncle Pastor, we can't!" wailed the robbers. "We don't want to hurt you!"

37

"Well, well!" said the traveller thoughtfully. "Then I shall have to pretend." Whereupon he promptly tumbled off the chair and rolled onto the floor, moaning and crying.

"Oh, my head! My poor, poor head!"

This brought Leni, who was supposed to be the priest who passed him by, screaming from the door. Tearing off the bathrobe that was her priest's robe, she fell on her knees beside the poor victim.

"I don't want to be a priest!" she sobbed. "I want to help my Uncle Pastor!"

"Of course you do! Of course. Of course," he comforted, picking himself and her off the floor. He looked around the room. Very quietly. The room became hushed and still.

"Children, you *know*," he said. "*You* know. You little children of Patmos know what Jesus is trying to tell us grownups because we do not know and have to be told."

His eyes crinkled with a smile. "Thank you," he said to every corner of the room.

It was then that he saw Gunther on Sister Mathilde's lap.

"Ah, I see we have a new one!" He plucked Gunther from Sister Mathilde's lap and sat down with him. The two looked at each other, looked deep into each other. Pastor Fritz looked and saw the boy within the stunted, twisted body. The boy within the stunted, twisted body looked and saw the man who did not see his stunted, twisted body, did not see it at all.

What happened then was invisible to all eyes, even the deeply seeing eyes of Pastor Fritz. Yet it was so powerful and overwhelming that it could almost be compared to an epileptic attack. Except that it was a rising up and not a falling down—a great light instead of a great darkness. In a wave there flooded over the boy a dim and jumbled but wildly wonderful realization of the possibility of life—that he was not a piece of human garbage carried along on a gray and endless tide of time. He could *be*. Time was for *being*. Time was for *becoming*. Time was for becoming

what he could be. His head rang with a thou[
notes. A thousand red checkered tablecloths[
mind.

"What is your name, my son?" asked Pastor Fritz.

"Gunther! My name is Gunther," he answered clearly.

THE LANGUAGE
OF PRAISE

In a way it can be said that for Gunther that first Sunday in August, 1921, was a self-sighting day. In another way it can be said that for him eternity entered into time on that day. From that day on Gunther's self began to be drawn in a steady curve around a center.

Not that Gunther suddenly realized all this! After all, he was only seven. What seven-year-old knows about discovering a self? Or about time and eternity. About eternity entering time. And Gunther's mind and spirit had suffered far more from lack of food for mind and spirit than his crippled body had suffered from lack of food. As a matter of fact, it was as if his mind and spirit had been blindfolded for seven years. Things with which most children are intimate—wind, stars, sand, mud, pebbles,

41

angleworms, butterflies—Gunther did not even know by name. Nor could he give any name to the strange and wonderful feeling awakened in him by the love he found in Bethel. He was seven years old, but he could not say, "I love you," for the word *love* was not in his vocabulary. Anyone who does not know the world of love cannot truly know and use the word for love. In Gunther's back room world there had been no sand, wind, stars, pebbles, angleworms, and butterflies. Or love.

But where it was too late for his body ever to grow and develop into what it was intended to be, it was not too late for his mind and spirit. The knowledge that Gunther discovered that day was that he was intended to be—and that it was not too late for him to become what he was intended to be. The difference between Gunther when he woke up in his Patmos bed on Monday morning and Gunther when he woke up on Sunday morning was that now with all his weak body and awakened mind and spirit he wanted to be. Wanted to be Gunther. The Gunther he had seen reflected in the eyes of Pastor Fritz. It was possible. Something or someone willed it. Now it was up to him, Gunther, to will it.

No one was happier for Gunther's new beginning than blind Willi. When Sister Mathilde came to dress Gunther and take him to breakfast, she found Willi already there, as excited as any tutor over a sudden transformation in a dull student.

"Tante Mathilde! I teached Gunther to talk. I teached Gunther to pray. Gunther, pray for Tante Mathilde."

"Or-r-r Fah-h--er hoo-oo is-s-s. . . ."

Gunther looked questioningly at his teacher.

"Our Father who is in heaven. *In heaven*, Gunther."

"Or-r-r Fah-h--er hoo-oo is-s-s in heff--en."

"Good, Gunther! Wonderful!" cried Sister Mathilde. Even Kurt in his next bed smiled wanly.

In his new beginning Gunther had little understanding

of the songs, hymns, psalms, prayers, and Bible verses his blind tutor taught him in the next months. Perhaps his teacher did not either! But for want of eyes, Willi was all ears and heart, and this was why he learned so much by ear and by heart.

"Oh--r oo-o-o orr Fah-h--er. in heff--en?" he asked the young deacon who carried him to the Beech Forest that day.

It took some time for the deacon to understand the strange sounds coming from Gunther's throat. When he did, he laughed heartily.

"No, Gunther. Just one of his many sons. And so are you. That means we are brothers. I am your Brother Herman. Can you say 'Brother Herman'?"

"Brudd--er Herr--man!" said Gunther triumphantly.

A few weeks later, when the way of speaking was more at home in his throat (although his throat, like his bones, never did learn to articulate perfectly), he quietly watched a strange man tenderly stroking Kurt's head.

"Arr oo Sun uff my soul thou Sav-i-or dear?" asked Gunther curiously.

"I beg your pardon?" asked the man, looking up from the pale, perspiring face, perspiring from yet another epileptic attack.

"Arr oo Sun uff my soul thou Sav-i-or dear?"

"Would that I were!" the strange man said sadly. "If I were I would take this poor suffering little soul to myself. No, I am the dear Savior's servant. I am Pastor Wilm. And who are you?"

"Gunther. My name is Gunther."

"God bless you, Gunther," said Pastor Wilm, placing his hand, still damp from Kurt's dark curls, on Gunther's brow. "Something tells me we are going to be very good friends."

Kurt, too, became Gunther's tutor, teaching him things blind Willi could not teach.

"What's this?" Gunther asked again and again, for

Gunther's brain, the master organ of his body because it had ten billion king-cells, was responding to his new will to be and was flashing orders from his mind to the approximately 480 muscles in his body.

"Stretch! Reach!" said the mind, and Gunther's brain flashed the message to the muscles. The muscles were stiff and stubborn at first. There was a battle between the stubborn muscles and the stubborn will. The will finally won, and Gunther's hand reached out and touched a moist, sluggish creature that promptly pulled back into a hard curved shell.

"What's this?" asked Gunther.

"Snail," said Kurt.

"Lift your right foot," said Gunther's mind, and the brain flashed the order to the muscles of the right leg. The same battle all over again. Again the will won, and the muscles of the right leg held the thin white crooked leg in a blob of amber light flickering through the canopy of branches. An insect with a slender body and four bright orange and black wings landed on his toe.

"What's that?" asked Gunther.

"Butterfly," said Kurt.

By now victory had gone to Gunther's head. "Get up and walk," ordered Gunther's mind, and Gunther's brain flashed the rash message to the muscles of his body. The aching muscles struggled with his rigid legs and arms and finally brought his body to a crouching position.

"Up! Up!" screamed the mind. "Get up!" Gunther's body lurched crazily up and pitched forward against the trunk of a century-old beech tree.

"Brother Herman!" screamed Kurt and Willi together.

"Not so fast, little brother," said Brother Herman, picking him up and carrying him back to Patmos House, where Sister Mathilde washed his bloody face.

"Absolutely not!" said Dr. Blümcke on his weekly visit. "No walking until your body is ready for it."

The doctor very wisely said nothing about creeping. It is true that man crawls before he walks, but in crawling a person places his hands palms down on the floor. Gunther's hands were permanently and rigidly bent downward and back under his wrist. No matter how sharp the commands Gunther's mind sent over the nerves to his hands and fingers, his hands and fingers would never help him crawl, do handsprings, grasp a cup, a spoon, a pencil.

But concepts, the idea of things, meanings—that was a different matter. Even if Gunther's hands could not grasp, his mind could. There was nothing crippled about the part of Gunther between his eyes and the lively center of his brain. There were health, soundness, law, and order in that kingdom. It had only been waiting for King Mind and Queen Will to wake up from their drowsy drugged sleep and to rule. Now that the royal pair, mind and will, had been awakened by the kiss of love, the ten million royal cells of the brain, the royal subjects of the mind and will, were ready to do.

"If we cannot get the body to walk," said King Mind and Queen Will, "then go fishing for words. Meanings! Meanings! We want all the meanings we can get."

The brain immediately spread its net and fished for concepts, ideas, and meanings.

The brain had wonderful fishing when Sister Mathilde carried Gunther to a little schoolroom in Patmos House where Sister Friedchen taught about ten children. There he learned numbers, and from then on his head was like a dovecote where numbers flew in and out. There in that schoolroom all the colors that had made him strangely happy, the red in the checkered tablecloth, the black and gold of the butterfly, got their proper names. He learned the vocabulary of relationships: near, far, up, down, inside, outside, above, under, more than, less than. The vocabulary of courtesy: please, thank you, good morning, good night, goodbye.

Here in this little schoolroom Gunther began learning the language which is very special to the Valley of Bethel. True, it is an international language and not just Bethel's alone. Every nation has some persons who know the language. Yet, again, it is not an inter-national language. It is a super-national language and has nothing at all to do with nations. It has to do with grateful hearts. Since Bethel was a valley full of very grateful hearts, it spoke this language fluently. That is, the language of praise.

One would think that in a valley where there is as much suffering as there is in the Valley of Bethel that the language spoken would be the language of complaint. In a place where there are at least forty epileptic attacks an hour, 1000 a day, 236,799 a year—in such a place one would expect to hear an everlasting chorus: "Why was I ever born?"

Even the healthy who live there and are constantly seeing these people whom the world of the well hides away because it does not want to see them—even they could be expected to be depressed and full of words of complaint and despair. "Our hearts bleed for these incurables. It's hopeless. Absolutely hopeless!" But the word "hopeless" is not in the language of praise which is spoken so fluently in the Valley of Bethel. Because the people who live in that valley know a love that has no limit, the voice of thanksgiving is stronger in that valley than the voice of complaint.

No one learned the special Bethel language of praise more quickly than Gunther. Having just come from a dreary, loveless back room to this bright valley of love, he could not learn it fast enough. He did not have to be pushed by his teachers at all. His mind and spirit were constantly being tugged and pulled. In fact, his mind and spirit ached as much to reach beyond themselves as the muscles of his body were aching because of all the stretching and reaching they were doing these days.

By mid-August Gunther had learned a praise verse from a psalm of David to recite to Pastor Fritz on his birthday. Pastor Fritz and his wife Julia were invited to all the houses in Bethel on their birthdays, but they always came to Patmos first, for the children in Patmos were first in their hearts. After the cherry cobbler birthday cake, the children sang songs and presented the pictures they had drawn and colored. Pastor Fritz lifted each child in his arms, laid his cheek against theirs. "Thank you, thank you, my Liebling!"

Those who could not talk wriggled and squirmed their joy. Some explored his bald head, moustache, and even his nostrils. Henrik, who could not control his fluttering hands, seemed to be hitting the birthday guest, which brought Leni out of the waiting line to his side.

"Don't you hurt my Uncle Pastor!" she said fiercely to Henrik.

"Those are love pats, my little friend," said Pastor Fritz, drawing Leni to his other knee. "The harder Henrik hits me, the louder he is saying he loves me."

"I love you awfully much, Uncle Pastor, but I don't want to hit you."

"You can hug me and kiss me."

"How old be you?"

"Forty-four."

"Then I kiss you forty-four times." Since Leni really could not count past four, she actually kissed him four times and then four more, which to her made forty-four.

Gunther thought the line would never move him up to Pastor Fritz. But what if he forgot his verse? When the rolling chair the men in Little Nazareth, the Carpenter House, had made for him finally reached the birthday guest, he had indeed forgotten. It wasn't a matter of muscles refusing to obey the mind's orders. The mind simply could not remember the words! Gunther sat speech-

47

less. None of his new vocabulary came to his rescue, not even the polite words. Not even "Happy Birthday!"

"Ah, it is you, Gunther! How fine you look! Julia, this is my new friend, Gunther. Gunther, this is my wife, Frau Julia."

Gunther's downcast eyes slowly raised to the face of a woman who wore her goodness as simply and naturally as she wore her homespun clothes. No doubt she had pinned her hair up neatly in the morning, but by now the knot had slipped and little strands were dangling in her neck. She never knew, because she never took time to look in the mirror. On that warm August day she looked as flushed and good as an apple, and just like an apple she was totally unconscious of how jolly and good and kind she looked.

Gunther's spirit did a triple somersault, and his mind suddenly remembered his gift to the honored guest: "I will bless the Lord at all times; his praise shall continually be in my mouth."

That was all Tante Friedchen had taught Gunther, but Pastor Fritz knew more. His voice continued the psalm in a ringing voice: "My soul makes its boast in the Lord; let the afflicted hear and be glad."

Frau Julia's voice picked up where he left off. Leaning toward Gunther and placing her hand on his twisted hand, she said as if saying it to him alone: "O magnify the Lord with me, and let us exalt his name together!"

Manfred, who had hundreds of facts and figures in his head but almost no meanings, was right behind Gunther.

"You were born August 14, 1877. You are 44. Ten years from now, 54. Twenty years, 64. Thirty years, 74."

"Manfred, Manfred," laughed Pastor Fritz. "Someday someone will invent a computer machine and pattern it after your mind."

"You see, children," cried a familiar voice, "I praise God with my trumpet. Manfred praises God with numbers."

Pastor Kuhlo, carrying his trumpet as if it were a third limb of his body, came through the door and stood behind Pastor Fritz and Frau Julia. "Manfred, please lead us in 44 Alleluias. The song goes like this, children.

> O friends, in gladness let us sing
> A song to Pastor Bodelschwingh!
> Alleluia! Alleluia!

Forty-four Alleluias, Manfred. No more, no less!"

Pastor Kuhlo put his trumpet to his lips, and laughter and loud alleluias filled the room—until Manfred yelled, "Forty-four!" Perhaps to some alien who did not know the language of praise the chorus might have sounded like a stuck record. To everyone there that day it was equal to if not greater than Handel's *Messiah*.

Only one child sang a forty-fifth Alleluia, and that was Monika, who in all her ten years had never before said a word. From that day on it was the only word in her vocabulary—until in another exciting songfest she learned "Hosannah." Only Monika pronounced it "Susannah." With these two words, "Loo-yah!" and "Susannah" she saluted the world in the morning. Many a night the Patmos children fell asleep to Monika singing her two words to melodies of her own composition.

By the end of his first month in Bethel so many fountains of meanings had sprung up in Gunther's mind that it must have looked like Niagara Falls under colored lights. Not all of them were tra-la-la fountains. One welled up and flowed in a quiet, sad undercurrent—the growing awareness that most of the children in Patmos and most of the patients in Bethel were sick in a different way than he was sick, the knowledge that sometime and somehow something had gone wrong inside their brain boxes.

What had gone wrong Gunther of course did not understand, but *that* something had gone wrong was very clear. He saw daily the signs and symptoms that his friends, the

49

first friends in his life, had suffered some pre-birth, in-birth, or after-birth misfortune in their brains.

There was Henrik, who could not control his movements, whose limbs twitched and trembled, whose hands and feet were hardly ever still. To feed him was a task that took infinite patience, for his head flopped from side to side. Sometimes his teeth clenched, and the Sister would have to wait until that spasm was over before she could put a spoon into his mouth. Half of the food dribbled back on the table. Instead of law and order, there was chaos inside Henrik's brain. Messages were flying in every wrong direction to the wrong muscles at the wrong time, producing muscular movements that Henrik, most of all, did not want.

Then there were Leni, Manfred, and many others of the Patmos children who could walk and talk and dress and feed themselves. But something was wrong in their brains, too, for all of them had epileptic attacks. "Fits" they were called. They came upon them as suddenly and unexpectedly as an enormous sneeze or an attack of hiccups. Only an instant of time separated being happy and well from— chaos.

Some had their epileptic attacks mildly. A funny feeling, a staring in the eyes. A grayout in the mind. Only for an instant.

Others had them more severely. Brownouts in the mind. Dizziness. Sagging head. Small jerkings and twitchings of the body.

Other epileptic fits Gunther saw daily were violent like earthquakes. A sudden shriek that many have compared to the raucous cry of a peacock. The body falls to the floor and twists and writhes. Total blackout in the mind. Complete anarchy in the brain. And the 480 muscles of the body are obedient to that total disobedience and mutiny in the mind. The body is in a convulsion.

But all of them, from the ones with the strongest bodies and minds to those with the weakest, all of them knew and understood the language of praise. Even deaf and dumb and very mentally retarded Dora, who could only squeal. One had only to look in her eyes to know that her squeals spelled sheer delight, for the eyes tell everything.

"I love you," her eyes said, "and I am the happiest of all people!"

There was one mind in Patmos House which disputed Dora's eyes, for that mind was positively certain that the happiest person in the whole world was a boy named Gunther.

THERE'S A CRACK
IN EVERYTHING

Of all Gunther's Patmos friends, it was Kurt who had the most frequent and most severe epileptic attacks. Each mind-quake left his body weaker and weaker. Yet of all the children in Patmos House it was Kurt who gave Gunther the richest gift—a home-sweet-home image, the vivid picture of a loving earthly home to hang on the bare walls of Gunther's mind.

Until the lights went out in the dormitory room, the two boys pressed their faces against the bars of their beds and talked. The one boy with his overflowing cup of home-love poured the home-feeling into the other boy's empty cup. Poured it so full that Gunther began to call Kurt's mother and father "Mommy" and "Daddy" as if they were his own.

"What was Mommy's name?" asked Gunther.

"Rachel. Sometimes Daddy called her 'Rachel, my Joy, my Jewel, my Jewess.' Then he would pick me up and hug me and call me Benjy."

"Why Benjy? Your name is Kurt."

So Kurt had to tell Gunther the Bible story about Jacob and Leah and Rachel and the twelve sons. Benjamin was the youngest. He was Jacob's pet because he was Rachel's son, and Jacob loved Rachel most of all.

"You see, Jacob and Isaac and Abraham are my forefathers."

"That's only three," said Gunther, proud to know his numbers.

"O, you silly!" laughed Kurt, and proceeded to tell Gunther what forefathers meant.

"Are Jacob, Isaac, and Abraham my forefathers, too?" asked Gunther.

"Not really, 'cause you're not Jewish. They weren't Daddy's either. He wasn't a Jew. But we celebrated all the Jewish holy days—Hanukkah, Purim, Passover. And all the Christian ones—Advent, Christmas, Easter. We celebrated all the time—Daddy, Mommy, and I. But Christmas most of all."

"What's Christmas?" asked Gunther.

Kurt sat up in bed, horrified. "You mean you don't even know what Christmas is?"

"We never celebrated anything," said Gunther, humbly.

Just then the lights went out.

"Do you think we'll celebrate Christmas here in Bethel?" whispered Gunther in the dark.

"Of course! Here at Bethel we celebrate everything! It's just like home. Go to sleep, Gunther. I'm tired."

But a little later Gunther heard Kurt whisper to himself, "Not just like home,"—crying softly. Gunther lay in the dark wondering. Was it better to have had a wonderfully loving home and to have lost it—or never to have had such a home. Soon he, too, was crying silently for the splendid

54

professor-daddy who was drafted toward the end of the war when everybody was drafted and was killed his very first day at the front. For the lovely mommy with dark curls like Kurt's who died in the flu epidemic after the war. For this beautiful Benjy-boy, who had also gotten the flu, and then got measles, and then got this falling sickness, and now was getting weaker and weaker.

Willi stood between the two beds early the next morning, as aware as Gunther, with his two good eyes, of Kurt's body in the powerful spasms of an early morning attack. When the body finally stopped tossing and twitching and lay limp and exhausted, when the mind had staggered out of its darkness, Kurt opened his eyes.

"I think I will go soon to Daddy and Mommy."

"No!" cried Gunther violently.

Willi turned his sightless face to him reprovingly.

"No say No! Heavenly home good place. Best of all place."

"I think I will be in the heavenly home by Christmas."

"No, no, no," sobbed Gunther.

"Gunther, I sing song 'bout heavenly home," said Willi, who had so few words in his vocabulary but so many songs in his heart.

> Jerusalem, my happy home,
> When shall I come to thee?
> When shall my sorrows have an end?
> Thy joys when shall I see?

"I *know* when!" said Kurt, his voice glad and strong. "At Christmas!"

Thus Gunther had two very opposite feelings as he approached his first real Christmas. It was like discovering a new star in the sky. First a pinpoint of light, growing bigger day by day, until at last it was the biggest and brightest star in the heaven. But it was also like discovering a dark cloud low on the horizon, and the cloud, too, grew bigger and bigger each day. All the time Gunther's idea of Christmas was growing little by little, his friend Kurt was dying little by little.

Not that the two clashing feelings in any way clashed with his daily joy over daily new discoveries. The tingling "I am alive, alive!" sensation he felt for the first time in Bethel grew with his "at home" feeling in Bethel. His body felt more and more inclined to move and stretch. Forbidden to walk, unable to crawl, he discovered other ways of locomotion. Rolling off the blanket in the Beech Forest one exceptionally warm, sunny autumn day he discovered the fun of rolling on dry, crinkled beech leaves and hearing them crunch. That same day he discovered a congregation of ladybugs settling down for the long winter.

"Look! Look!" he shouted, "Manfred can't count these many!" It was true. For once Manfred did not have enough numbers in his mind. The statistical machine in his brain broke down before the ladybugs.

Gunther's two conflicting feelings about Christmas almost rubbed each other out on the First Sunday in Advent. By three o'clock the fear feeling had practically vanished. Up until that time everything was new and excitingly wonderful. Instead of the wake-up bell, the Patmos Sisters, each carrying a lighted candle, walked through all the sleeping rooms singing the beautiful Advent hymn by Paul Gerhard:

> O how shall I receive thee,
> How greet thee, Lord, aright?
> All nations long to see thee,
> My Hope, my heart's delight!
> O kindle, Lord most holy,
> Thy lamp within my breast,
> To do in spirit lowly
> All that may please thee best.

Then from the Zion Church hilltop came the sound of Pastor Kuhlo's brass choir playing "Lift up your heads, ye mighty gates, Behold the King of glory waits!" To be sure that everyone, absolutely everyone, in every house in Bethel heard that stirring music, they marched down the hill to Old Ebenezer, the first house in Bethel, then up steep Jägerbrink past Sarepta, the Deaconess Mother House, up the hill to Bethelweg, down the hill again on Saronweg. In front of Patmos House the brass choir stopped and played the children's carol, "O come, little children, O come, one and all."

The tangy smell of evergreen branches filled every room in Patmos House that morning. Every room had an Advent wreath with four white candles, one for each Sunday in Advent. The largest wreath hung over the center table in the large dining room. The first candle in this wreath was not lit until Pastor Fritz came after their naptime. Gunther saw at once that it was not to be the usual Bible story time, for Frau Julia was along, carrying a basket trimmed with red ribbons. The basket proved to be full of gingerbread stars, a silver candy tipping each of the five points of the star.

The mood of the Patmos children was already pitched very high by the events of the day. Perhaps too high. Now that Uncle Pastor and Frau Pastor had come, their cries became almost ear-splitting. As Pastor Fritz and Frau Julia sat down before the Advent wreath, the jubilation soared. Without any one child's willing it, but with each child fanning the other's jubilant mood, the room began to sound like a rumpus room.

"Shh! Children, children, be quiet!" cried the Patmos Sisters in alarm, jumping up wherever they were sitting. But the pitch of jubilation-out-of-bounds climbed another degree. Pastor Fritz covered his face with his hands, bowed his head upon the table. The noise simmered down to silence. Before it could became a silence as prodigal as the previous noise, Pastor Fritz raised his head, smiled. There was not a sound in the room.

"Ah, children, now I can hear Advent! You see, Advent is a time of stillness when we prepare our hearts for the Christchild's birth. I should like to teach you a prayer today. It is by Martin Luther, who wrote this song for his own dear children. Listen carefully, now!

> Ah, dearest Jesus, Holy Child,
> Make thee a bed, soft undefiled,
> Within my heart, that it may be
> A quiet chamber kept for thee.

Obediently they said it after him. When they had learned it as well as they could, they sang it with folded hands and bowed heads.

When Gunther raised his head from singing the prayer, the fear feeling had completely vanished. Or so he thought. Perhaps that is why the joy feeling crashed and smashed as suddenly as it did.

"Sister Friedchen, who is going to light the first Advent candle in the wreath this year?" asked Pastor Fritz.

"We think Kurt should do it this year," answered Sister Friedchen. She picked Kurt from the wagon in which he was pulled about now that he was too weak to walk and placed him in Pastor Fritz's arms. The shiny bald head bowed to the dark curly head and ruddy cheek lay for a moment against pale, pinched cheek.

"Benjamin, my child! O, my little Benjy!"

The boy looked up in wonder. His hand crept up to Pastor Fritz's face and felt the wetness there.

"My Daddy called me that! How did you know?" he whispered, his dark eyes shining.

The children watched expectantly as Kurt took a small lighted candle from Sister Friedchan's hand and leaned toward the tall unlighted candle of the Advent wreath. But before the flame of the one candle touched the wick of the other, the burning candle dropped. A sucking-in-moan burst from Kurt's lips, and his body writhed in spasm after spasm. Sister Friedchen swiftly took him in her arms and left the room.

Frau Julia had rescued the candle, and Pastor Fritz calmly lit the tall candle, singing the prayer song as he did. Frau Julia and the Sisters joined him. The candle caught the flame, and the singing grew stronger as now one and now another child chimed in. But a shrill cry from the top of Gunther's lungs and the bottom of his suddenly returned fear and misery silenced the song.

"There's a crack in everything!"

Every face in the room turned and looked at Gunther, but Gunther looked only at one face. Once again he flung his wild, desperate complaint against that face.

"There's a crack in everything!"

Now every face in the room looked at Pastor Fritz, expectantly. Pastor Fritz looked at Gunther, and for a moment it seemed as if the tons and tons of pain and suffering concentrated in the little valley of Bethel were crushing him.

For Gunther the joyous expectation of Christmas feeling was practically rubbed out by the other, the fear feeling. His complaint turned into a cry for help: "What's so great about Christmas?"

The little candle slanted toward the table and dripped a steady stream of wax. Frau Julia reached for it, blew it out, and took the hand in hers. The hand gripped hers tightly.

The silence ached with Gunther's pain and the Patmos children's pain. Their pain was not Gunther's pain, but they knew instinctively that Gunther's pain had entered into their beloved Uncle Pastor.

"Children," he said at last, turning from Gunther to them, appealing directly to them, and each one felt the directness of his appeal. "Gunther wants to know what is so great about Christmas. Gunther *needs* to know what is so great about Christmas. And I need you to help me tell him. Will you please help me?"

Too weak and flawed to hear Gunther's cry for help, the minds of the Patmos children nevertheless could hear Uncle Pastor's appeal for help. They earnestly set their poor brains to work the best their poor damaged brains knew how. Such an appeal, they knew, could not be answered just from the top of the brain.

Manfred was the first to stand and offer the work of his brain. "Christmas comes in December. December is the twelfth month. Christmas comes the twenty-fifth day. The twenty-fifth day of the twelfth month."

"So it does. Thank you, Manfred," said Pastor Fritz, and Manfred sat down.

Monika jumped to her feet and beamed at Pastor Fritz. "Loo-yah! Susannah!" she sang, and sat down.

"Thank you, Monika," said Pastor Fritz. "Can anyone else tell Gunther what is so great about Christmas?"

Far down the table rose Petra, the oldest of the Patmos patients, thirty-five years old, but five years young in mind. She had remained at Patmos to be a faithful helper with the small children, and now again she was offering her help. After all, she had heard the story many times over.

"Christmas so great 'cause then God sent his Son Jesus our Savior."

"That is true, Petra. Thank you. But *why?* Why, children, did God send his Son to be our Savior?"

Willi, having ransacked all the hymns he knew by heart, jumped up. "To ransom captive Israel!" he cried.

"Very good, Willi. Thank you." But Pastor Fritz still waited for an answer he seemed to expect.

Leni, who had covered her face with her hands and laid it on the table in perfect imitation of her Uncle Pastor, beat and cudgled her brains. Why, oh why did God send his Son at Christmas? And finally in that dim brain box a great light burst. Leni climbed from her chair to the table.

"Because," she shouted triumphantly, "Because everything has a crack!"

Pastor Fritz strode to Leni's side and gathered her into his arms. From that lofty perch she could kiss the top of his head ecstatically. Pastor Fritz knelt beside Gunther's chair. Their eyes met. By the same path that pain had sped from one to the other, a radiant trust returned.

"It is true, Gunther, that there is a crack in everything. God sees the crack better than we do, and the crack is ever so much worse than we think it is. That is why God sent his Son from the heavenly home to our earthly home. Not to patch up the crack, but to make everything new. That is why Christmas is so great, Gunther."

With the arm and hand that was not holding Leni, Pastor Fritz picked up Gunther's right hand. "This hand will never be able to write, Gunther, but your mind is strong and sound and true. I shall pray God's Holy Spirit to take you by the hand of your mind, guide the hand of your mind, and patiently spell out the full meaning of Leni's great answer to your very good question. Thank you for asking it, Gunther. Thank you for answering it, Leni."

The days of Advent marched toward Christmas, full of the promises of God to bring comfort to the afflicted, full of music and happy Christmas activities. The whole valley of Bethel was caught up in preparing for the great festival. House parents visited the Christmas House next to Brockensammlung again and again to find just the right gift for the right person in their house-family. Some of the patients melted old wax and made new candles. Others cleaned and polished candle holders. All the choirs—voice, brass, and mouth organ—practiced twice as much and as hard as usual. The woodcutters cut evergreen branches for decorating, and a tree for each house and two tall trees for Zion Church. The gardeners decorated the chancel. And the children in Patmos House made yards and meters of paper chains.

Gunther could not make paper chains, but he could learn

the promise verses and the Advent songs and Christmas carols. Thanks to his self-appointed tutor, blind Willi, he learned them all from beginning to end. In the early evening before the lights went out he sang them softly to Kurt.

On the fourth Sunday in Advent Sister Mathilde took Kurt away to sleep in a little room next to her own so that she could watch him more closely through the long December nights. But on December 22, when the Patmos children marched into the brightly lighted dining room singing "O come, all ye children," they found him resting on a pillow in a wagon beside Pastor Fritz. In front of Pastor Fritz was a Christmas crèche, complete with Mary, Joseph, the Baby, the stable animals, the shepherds, the Wise Men, the angels, and the star. To many of the Patmos children, the figures by now were as familiar as the story, but they leaned toward the crèche and the story more eagerly than to the table loaded with a gift for each one and covered with a great white tablecloth.

"May I please have Kurt closest to me tonight when I tell you the story about the Christchild?" asked Pastor Fritz. "This is Kurt's last Christmas with us, you know."

The children nodded quietly. They all knew it was Kurt's last Christmas with them. Gunther knew it, too, but there no longer was any fear in his knowing.

"And may I also have Gunther close to me when I tell the story, for this is Gunther's first Christmas with us."

Finally, at long last, all the bits and pieces Gunther had been hearing about Christmas all through Advent, the whole jigsaw puzzle of Christmas, fell into place. No one could tell the story better than Pastor Fritz. Lifting each carved figure, he glowingly placed it into the crèche of the Patmos children's minds. Poor and humble though the stables of their minds were, they were large enough to receive the whole multitude of animals, angels, and people. The Patmos children were deficient in mind but not in adoration. They were perfectly able to arrange the figures of the Christmas crèche in an adoring circle around the Son of God. There are some who say that the very poverty of their minds makes this miracle possible.

So vividly were the crude figures transformed into vivid presences in the Patmos children's minds that when Pastor Fritz picked up the figure of the Christchild, Leni could not contain herself any longer. "And now Christ our Savior is born!" she cried.

"Loo-yah! Loo-yah! Susannah! Susannah!" sang Monika.

When the tablecloth was removed from the gift table, there was another kind of jubilation. Everyone knew what it was all about—that is, everyone but Gunther. Never in his life had he received a gift. Even when he saw his friends go up to the gift table and receive a gift—Leni a teddybear, Monika a doll, Willi a mouth organ—he could not imagine that there would be anything for him. Not even when he heard his name called and Sister Mathilde pushed him to the table and a gaily painted train was placed in his lap, not even then could he believe that this was *his* train, his own personal, private possession. That he, too, could squeal with joy and shout as the others did, "Look! Look! See what I got for Christmas!" Gunther touched each car of the train—engine, coal car, mail car, passenger car, caboose. They could be hooked together—and unhooked. Had real wheels that turned. He could lie on his stomach on the floor and push the train around in circles.

"Gunther! Gunther! Where are you?" called Willi, groping around in the happy crowd. "Look what I got for Christmas—a mouth organ!"

"Over here, Willi!" shouted Gunther. "See what I got—a train!"

Suddenly Gunther thought of Kurt. Had Kurt received a Christmas gift? If not, should he give him his train? By jerking his chair and with Willi pushing he made his way back to Kurt, who lay on his pillow looking rapturously at a Mother and Child figure delicately carved from olive wood. Where had Gunther seen that carving before? Yes, it was the one he had seen in Sister Mathilde's room. Gunther's eyes met Sister Mathilde's, and she ever so slightly shook her head.

"She is so beautiful—the Mother Mary!" said Kurt. "Just like Mommy!"

On Christmas Eve day Gunther forgot about Kurt and his wish to go to the heavenly home for Christmas. Sister Anna fed him his oatmeal porridge at breakfast because Tante Mathilde, she said, was busy. Between spoonfuls she told him that all the Patmos children who were strong enough would go to Christmas Vespers in Zion Church that evening. Brother Herman had promised to carry Gunther and lead Willi. There was nothing more beautiful, said Sister Anna, than the Vesper service in Zion Church on Christmas Eve. Every candle on the twin trees in the chancel was lighted. And Pastor Fritz brought messages from Bethel's friends all over the world. Last year he had read the letter from America telling about the cows that were going to be sent.

"And now, Gunther, here's a cup of milk from that Christmas present to the children of Bethel."

All morning Gunther played with his train and Willi practiced "Silent Night, Holy Night" on his mouth organ. Just before the noon meal Sister Mathilde came into the room, pulling Kurt on a wagon.

"Kurt asked me to bring him to you. He wants to say goodbye to you now because he knows that he is leaving us soon to go to his heavenly home. Will you all come and bid Kurt goodbye?"

Willi was the first. "Kurt, you my friend. I play 'Silent Night, Holy Night' for you."

"No, Willi," said Sister Mathilde gently. "Kurt is too tired to hear you play. He just wants to touch you and say goodbye."

It was as simple as that. A touch—and a goodbye.

"Goodbye, Willi."

"Goodbye, Kurt. You my friend."

"Goodbye, Leni."

"Goodbye, Kurt."

Perhaps Kurt's fingers clung a bit longer to Gunther's hand. But if he had any special last message, he was too weak to say it.

"Goodbye, Gunther."

"Goodbye, Kurt. Greet Mommy and Daddy!"

Just before Brother Herman came to take him and Willi to Christmas Eve Vespers, Tante Mathilde came into the room. "Our Kurt has now gone to the Christmas Room in heaven. He said that we are not to be sad."

But sad tears nevertheless did trickle down Brother Herman's collar as he carried Gunther up the hill.

"Gunther," said Brother Herman. "Cry your tears and do not be ashamed. Tears, too, are a gift of love. But think of how rich you are to have had such a friend. And think of how rich we all are that Jesus Christ came from the heavenly home to live among us as a friend."

On the second day of Christmas, Pastor Fritz put it all together—the sadness and the gladness. On that day the Patmos children said a final goodbye to the body of their friend. In no way at all was it a fearsome or a gruesome thing to be near the dead body of someone they loved. Every child who could hold a candle held one. Each one placed his lighted candle before the simple pine casket where Kurt lay as if sleeping, his hands folded around his Christmas gift, the olive wood carving of the Mother and Child. Pastor Kuhlo blew *"O du Fröliche"* on his trumpet, and the children sang that carol about Christmas joy as if death were not in the room at all. Then Pastor Fritz stood by the coffin and spoke. For what seemed like a long time he looked down at the boy who though pale as wax seemed to be only sleeping.

"Kurt was not with us very long," he said, touching the

dark curls. "But every time I saw this beautiful little boy I thought to myself, Jesus must have looked like this. You see, children, Kurt's mother was a Jew. And Jesus our Savior was a Jew. He could very well have looked like our Kurt."

Pastor Fritz raised his eyes from the coffin and searched the room until he found Gunther. "Kurt wished to go to the heavenly home. I think he was homesick for the heavenly home because his home here on earth was so dear to him. You were his friends, and you saw that he had no fear at all about dying. And this is what is so great about Christmas. We need have no fear of dying when our Savior Jesus Christ has been born. Because Jesus left his heavenly home and came to us at Christmas, our friend Kurt could leave his earthly home without any fear. This is the priceless treasure of Christmas."

Pastor Kuhlo softly played a chorale, and the Patmos children and the deaconesses and deacons sang it. *"Jesu, meine Freude"* it is called in German, "Jesus my Joy."

> Jesus, priceless Treasure,
> Source of purest pleasure,
> Truest friend to me;
> Long my heart hath panted,
> Till it well-night fainted,
> Thirsting after thee.
> Thine I am, O spotless Lamb,
> I will suffer nought to hide thee,
> Ask for nought beside thee.
>
> In thine arm I rest me;
> Foes who would molest me
> Cannot reach me here.
> Though the earth be shaking,
> Every heart be quaking,
> God dispels our fear;

Sin and hell in conflict fell
With their heaviest storms assail us:
Jesus will not fail us.

Hence, all thoughts of sadness!
For the Lord of gladness,
Jesus, enters in;
Those who love the Father,
Though the storms may gather,
Still have peace within;
Yea, whate'er we here must bear,
Still in thee lies purest pleasure,
Jesus, priceless Treasure!

Gunther had heard many hymns since he came to Bethel the first of August, but never had any hymn made the impression upon him that this hymn did. The music was slow, stately, overpowering. But the words, the words! They said it all! Everything Pastor Fritz had said from the first time he took his crippled body into his arms and looked deep into his being. Everything he had said today over Kurt's still body. Oh, to know hymns like that, every word of them! Oh, to be able to sing hymns like that to others so that they, too, would know what the hymn was saying.

Hence, all thoughts of sadness!
For the Lord of gladness,
Jesus, enters in.

Today he had not even been able to hold a lighted candle and place it before Kurt's coffin. But his mind could do what his hands could not. He *could* learn hymns. Lots of them. That he could do—and he would. Yes, he would. And sing them. He would never sing like a nightingale. More like a crow, no doubt. But if he could sing well enough so that people heard the great words—!

Gunther looked up as if from a dream awakening. His eyes rested on Kurt in his coffin. "Kurt," he whispered, "I am not sad anymore. You are with the Lord of gladness, and I am glad."

And that was Gunther's first Christmas at Bethel.

I CAN READ

The Christmas trimmings, stars, candleholders, and crèches were put away. A new boy lay in Kurt's bed, but the new boy could do nothing but turn his head, and there was no brightness in his eyes.

To Gunther's surprise, on the morning that Patmos school was to start again, Sister Mathilde did not wheel him to his usual corner in the school room but to the room where she wrote letters and received visitors.

"Gunther," she said, "I have a happy surprise for you. From now on you will go to school in Hebron. Patmos School is much too easy for you."

Gunther's face puckered with alarm. "But—but, I *like* it here! I don't want to go to another school. Please, Tante Mathilde, don't make me go!"

The crisp white bow under Sister Mathilde's chin moved comfortingly closer. "Gunther, dear child, you really should never have come to Patmos at all. Since you did not talk, it was thought that your mind was afflicted as the minds of most of our Patmos children are afflicted. But your mind is strong and sound. It can learn much, very much. The boys at Hebron have epileptic attacks, but their minds are not badly hurt. With them you will learn everything that children learn in schools all over Germany. You will learn to read, Gunther. Just think of it! You will learn to read books!"

Gunther did think about it. He thought of his school-mates in the Patmos schoolroom. Of restless, fidgety August who pinched his ear every time Sister Friedchen wasn't looking. Of the boy who did nothing but sit in the farthest corner and hum to himself. Of the highest achievement of a whole week for some of the children—to pick out all the red beads from a box of many-colored beads and make a chain of them.

"I will go to Hebron if I may always come back here."

Because it was January, Gunther was bundled up warmly. Because it had snowed in the night, he was transported from Patmos to Hebron in a sled. Because Sister Anna, who pulled the sled, was young and gay, she trotted him down Saronweg and up Hebronweg to the beautiful old farm-house that had been bought for Bethel in 1879 and now served as a schoolhouse and dining room for epileptic boys of school age.

A deacon brother carried Gunther into Old Hebron, deposited him in a homemade wheelchair, and rolled him into the low-ceilinged schoolroom, bright and cheerful because of its many casement windows.

School had started at eight o'clock, and Gunther was late. Mr. Kunze, the teacher, greeted him briefly with, "Aha, a new bird!" and motioned the brother to wheel his chair over by the window nearest to him.

Gunther felt strangely comforted when he remembered that Pastor Kuhlo had introduced him to the Patmos children by saying, "See, my little birds, I have brought you another little warbler to sing praises with you." His eyes darted nervously about the room, dropped shyly before the direct and curious stares of the twenty boys seated at double desks. Only one other boy was in a wheelchair. No girls. All boys. And yes, Sister Mathilde was right, they were different from the Patmos children. A feeling of panic clutched his mind.

"There are birds and birds," said Mr. Kunze cheerfully, walking with a bouncing step back and forth in front of the room. "Barnyard birds—hens, roosters, geese. Some of you gentlemen have had the honor of being chased by the Hebron geese."

This brought nods and loud laughter from the boys.

"In fact, gentlemen, do you know that Old Hebron was once called the 'Chicken Farm'? The counts who lived in the Sparrenberg Castle right outside Bethel kept the chickens they collected from the peasants as a kind of tax here on this farm.

"And then there are the birds of prey—owls, hawks, eagles, falcons. The Count of Ravensberg, you may be sure, did a lot of hunting with falcons.

"But today our lesson is about the singing birds we hear in this area. Now maybe you think it's crazy to have a lesson on singing birds in January. But in my opinion it's best to have a lesson on singing birds when we miss them the most. Does anyone recognize this songbird?"

Gunther could hardly believe his ears. In fact, he did quickly look about to see if a real bird really was in the room, but it truly was Mr. Kunze whistling!

"The wren!" several boys shouted at once.

"Good! And here's a picture of that tiny little songstress. Pass it around, boys. And right after it comes a picture of the gold-crested wren. The Scandinavians have a wonderful legend about a great competition among the birds to see which one could fly the highest. The bird that could fly the highest was to be crowned the King of the Birds. Which bird was crowned king do you think?"

"The eagle."

"No, indeed! It was a little wren. A little wren quietly sat on the eagle's back. The eagle flew up and up toward the sun until it was exhausted. But the little wren darted from his back and shot up still higher. So high, so close to the sun, that its head got burned by the scorching rays and the wren plummeted to earth. But it had gone the highest and was crowned the King of the Birds. But forever after that bird has had a yellow-gold crest. Now, who can name the Scandinavian countries and point to them on the map?"

This done, Mr. Kunze whistled another birdsong. "Which bird is this?"

"The blackbird!"

"Correct! We who live in Europe think that the blackbird is as beautiful a singer as the skylark and the nightingale. The English—where do the English live? Correct! The English have a poem about Old King Cole, a merry old soul, and a merry old soul was he. He sat down to a bird pie, and when the pie was opened, the birds began to sing. Four and twenty blackbirds they were. But American children—who can point to the country they live in? American children just can't understand that poem. Singing blackbirds! The only blackbirds they know are rude, ill-behaved birds that just raise a hubbub of screeches. Our blackbird is a singing thrush. The Americans have singing thrushes, but none of them is a black bird."

The hour sped by as if it were but ten minutes. On and on went Mr. Kunze, whistling bird songs, passing around pictures, telling fascinating stories about each bird—the blue titmouse, the marsh titmouse, the redstart, the robin.

The Americans have a robin, too, but it is larger than our robin. Our European robins have red pants as well as a red breast. But now—outside with you! You have fifteen minutes to be snowbirds. When you come back, we'll have arithmetic problems about Old King Cole's blackbirds."

"What about me?" wondered Gunther when the twenty boys rushed out sounding like twice-twenty. The old panic feeling started to come back, but Mr. Kunze pushed him up to his desk.

"There, my boy, now we two can have a little chat. What is your name, please?"

"My name is Gunther."

"Can you read, Gunther?"

"No, Sir."

"Would you like to read?"

"O, yes, Sir!"

"Fine! No better time to start than now. Pick out two bird pictures you like best."

Mr. Kunze spread the pictures out on his desk, and Gunther pointed to the gold-crested wren and the blackbird. Mr. Kunze printed some words carefully on the lower margin below the pictures and pushed them in front of Gunther.

"Take these pictures back to Patmos. The words under the wren say: 'I am Gunther. I see the bird.' The words under the blackbird say: 'The bird sings. The bird sings to me.'"

When Sister Anna brought him back to Patmos at noon, Gunther shouted to anyone and everyone within earshout, "I can read! I can read!" When they crowded around him he carefully placed the cards on his knees and read, pausing dramatically between each word.

> I am Gunther.
> I see the bird.
> The bird sings.
> The bird sings to me.

When Sister Mathilde put Gunther to bed that night,

she put an open Bible on his knees. "Here in the first three lines of Psalm 96 you will find a word you learned today. Once in each line. Can you tell me what it is?"

Gunther frowned at the small print. "I see a word three times. It's—it's—*sings!* What do all the words say?"

Sister Mathilde pointed to each word and said it aloud. Gunther's mind swallowed each new word hungrily. At his request she left the Bible with him, left him reading over and over to the new boy with no brightness in his eyes.

> O sing to the Lord a new song;
> Sing to the Lord, all the earth!
> Sing to the Lord, bless his name.

A month later Gunther's happy new song, "I can read! I can read!" suddenly was drowned out by the terrified old song. But even though his body was much stronger now, his wail of dismay and fear was muted. "No, no, I don't want to! I don't want to!" he sobbed when Sister Mathilde told him that it had been decided that he should move to New Hebron and live with the boys with whom he went to school. "I love you, Tante Mathilde. I love Willi and Leni and Monika. I even love August a little bit. I don't know any of the boys at Hebron."

"That's just the trouble, Gunther. We rush you there to school, we rush you back for dinner, and you don't get to know them."

"I don't want to know them!"

"Pastor Kuhlo is the house pastor there. You will see much more of him, learn ever so many more hymns."

"I don't care!"

Sister Mathilde's voice edged with sternness. "Very well, Gunther, if you will not go to Hebron for good reasons, then go in obedience. Pastor Bodelschwingh asked that you be moved from Patmos to Hebron."

"He did?"

"Yes, he did!"

"Pastor Fritz wants me to move to Hebron?"

"Yes, he does."

"Well," sighed Gunther, "then there is nothing to do but go to Hebron."

Obediently, but most unwillingly, Gunther moved to Hebron that evening. No farewell, not even Kurt's, was sadder than his farewell to his Patmos friends. But no welcome could have been warmer than the welcome given him by the houseparents, Father and Mother Mast. No one, not even the Tante Sisters, could have prepared him for bed more tenderly than had Brother Thomas, one of the young deacons assigned to Hebron. Nevertheless, Gunther lay with his face turned to the wall and wept silently. He did not even turn to hear what Brother Thomas was reading to the boys before the lights went out.

The story that night happened to be "Daniel in the Lions' Den." When Brother Thomas got to the part that said, "Then the king commanded, and Daniel was brought and cast into the den of lions," the boy nearest Gunther burst out laughing.

"Gunther is crying. Gunther is scared. Gunther thinks he has been thrown into a den of lions. We are lions, Gunther! Grr! Grr! Grrrrr!"

Whereupon there was such an uproar of snarling and growling in the room that Father Mast came running. "What's the matter here?"

Brother Thomas quickly explained. Father Mast strode to Gunther's bed, turned and faced the other boys, still struggling to stifle their mirth over their own cleverness.

"Have you forgotten already what it is to be homesick? That for a time it is a real *sickness*? I'm surprised, for some of you have just come to Bethel."

"But Gunther does not come from home," said the boy nearest to Gunther. "He's been living with the sillies at Patmos House."

"Feebs!" said another voice.

"Idiots!" cried someone from the other side of the room.

Gunther suddenly sat up in bed, and the roar that came from his mouth would have made a den of lions pause and take notice.

"They are not sillies, feebs, and idiots! They are my friends!"

Father Mast's chuckle broke the stunned silence.

"Good for you, my little Samson. You see, boys, Gunther has an advantage over you. He has lived at Patmos House and knows the children there. They are his kith and his kin. When I was just about your age I heard our Pastor Fritz's father say, 'Who is my closest relative? Who is nearest and dearest to me? The one who suffers most!' I have never forgotten that. This is the secret of true relationship. It is the secret of Bethel. Gunther has already learned that secret. Apparently you boys have not. Maybe Little Samson here can teach you. Goodnight Samson. Goodnight, lions. Mind you, no more roaring!"

After the lights went out, Gunther heard a whisper from the next bed.

"Gunther?"

"Yes?"

"My name is Klaus. I'm sorry!"

"It's O.K.," answered Gunther. "Who was Samson?"

"He was the strongest man in the world. He killed a lion with his bare hands. We'll ask Brother Thomas to read the story tomorrow night."

Gunther fell asleep, feeling that somehow everything was really going to be O.K., after all. He cried no more for Patmos House that night and very seldom again.

FAITH
SPREADS ITS WINGS

How could any boy moan for any past when the present was such jolly fun? When Mother Mast was such a good cook and made the best potato dumplings in the world? When Father Mast was the kind of a houseparent who made you feel like clapping instead of cringing when he entered the room? When the Brothers, who were as tender as mothers when someone had an attack, played with them in the afternoon as roughly as big brothers? When Pastor Kuhlo came at least every other day? When Mr. Kunze made knowledge sparkle and learning as pleasant as eating Mother Mast's dumplings? In fact, after a morning of school with him, you could almost hear your mind smacking its lips.

And with boys who were such—such lovable rogues!

"Sheep in wolves' clothing," Mr. Kunze called them after they had secretly slipped three white mice in his desk drawer. Although he was fond of everything in nature, he was not fond of mice and was most properly and appropriately surprised and scandalized. The boys' loud laughter turned into groans, however, when he coldly informed them that they would have school all afternoon that day instead of the usual 8:00 to 11:30.

Klaus, as spokesman for the boys, complained to Father Mast. "We think the punishment is too great for the crime."

"What do you suggest?" asked Father Mast, soberly. "Do the real culprits wish to confess and be birched in front of the whole class?"

The boys rose from their daily two-hour rest period after dinner—which was bad enough—and glumly filed across from New Hebron to Old Hebron. It was such a lovely day, too, with a feel of spring in the air—shirt-sleeve weather.

Mr. Kunze stood outside the closed door of the schoolroom, his arms grimly folded across his chest.

"Are you all here?" he asked curtly.

"Yes, Sir!"

"Line up, then. Heinz! Franz! Get your heads up! When I open the door, march to your desks and get to work. And not a peep out of you! Do you hear?"

"Yes, Sir!"

Mr. Kunze flung open the door and stood as stiff and straight as the door itself as they marched by.

"Mr. Kunze!" the first ones in the room shouted in amazement. "What does this mean?"

For there behind Mr. Kunze's desk stood the beaming houseparents, Pastor Kuhlo, and all the Brother-deacons. On the teacher's desk was a great bouquet of budding birch branches, forced in the garden-house by the Bethel gardeners. And on each desk were two gayly decorated cupcakes.

"It simply means," said Pastor Kuhlo, "that it is Mr. Kunze's birthday, and he wants to celebrate it with you little mice." He put his trumpet to his lips and played "All the birds are here again," but instead of the familiar words the houseparents and the deacons sang "All the mice are here again." The boys were unable to sing, they were laughing so hard.

After the cocoa and cake, Mr. Kunze sat on a high stool and read them a marvelous tale about the rats and mice in Hamelin town and a Pied Piper who piped them to their death in the River Weser, and of children who followed the Pied Piper into a great mountain and were never seen again. Only one boy was left behind—a little crippled lad who could not keep up with the others.

"Let's play the story!" cried Franz. "We have a Pied Piper and a cripple, Pastor Kuhlo and Gunther."

And so they did. The rats and mice were all drowned in the pond alongside Hebronweg. Then the rats and mice turned into children and noisily followed the Pied Piper up the climbing streets. In every house they passed, people flocked to the windows to see what was going on down there in the street. The children waved at them and shouted, "Goodbye! Goodbye! We're going to the Happy Land!"

"Where there is no more pain!" shouted Gunther, who with Klaus pushing his wheelchair was last of all in the procession.

Pied Piper Kuhlo led the children to the top of the hill and to the doors of Zion Church.

"You see," he said to them when they had all arrived, even Gunther and Klaus, "I have not brought you to a door in a mountain that will close behind you forever. I have brought you to Zion, the Heavenly City and the Kingdom of Eternal Love. Here no one is shut out, not even the little cripple who comes last."

And with that the Pied Piper waved his trumpet at them and disappeared with hurrying feet.

For Gunther, House Hebron proved to be Happy Land indeed. Sheltered and surrounded by love, he and his comrades in the next few years were not aware of the very difficult times that Bethel—indeed, all Germany—was going through. No one told them that in the Bethel Counting House the clerical staff was by no means as merry as Old King Cole when the figures they worked with soared from millions to milliards to billions to trillions. German money was worthless in those years. Waste baskets were no longer big enough to hold the worthless money, and laundry baskets were used. The men who were trying to keep Bethel going drew money from the banks in the big cities of Düsseldorf, Kiel, Kassel, and Wiesbaden and hurried to Bethel to pay it out the same day before it, too, lost its value. The inflation grew, year by year. The price of a pair of shoes went from 25 marks to 25 hundred marks to 25 thousand marks to 25 million.

Needless to say, banks, factories, businesses, and institutions, unable to operate with worthless money, closed their doors. Needless to say, too, the needs were greater now than ever. Thousands of men tramped from here to there on the roads of Germany, not because they had the wanderlust but because they had lost their jobs. On the heels of hunger came sickness. Yet many of the institutions that wanted to help people in need also had to close their doors.

Bethel, too, was urged to close its doors by some who had lost all hope. But instead, Bethel opened its doors to the crowds of homeless.

"When human thinking has come to a dead end and can see no way out of its problems," said Pastor Fritz calmly, "then faith is able to spread its wings. The climate has never been better—for faith."

Pastor Fritz's calm trust and faith did take wings. When things were at their worst in Bethel and many were becoming ill from lack of sufficient food, Christians in Switzerland, Holland, Sweden, Great Britain, and the United States began sending food.

For the boys at Hebron the only inkling—and it was only

an inkling—that anything was wrong in the years 1922 through 1924 was that there was not as much food as usual. Boys seem to have bottomless stomachs anyway, and boys with epilepsy even more so.

Being boys, they grumbled a bit. "Mother Mast isn't as good a cook as she used to be," or, "I hope nobody comes and stays for dinner today."

One afternoon Pastor Fritz, taking a shortcut through his back yard, found Heinz and Franz sitting under an apple tree. When he came by two hours later, they were still sitting there.

"What on earth are you doing, boys?" he asked in surprise.

"Waiting."

"Waiting for what?"

"For an apple to fall. Father Mast says we are not to *steal* apples from any tree in Bethel. But if an apple *falls* by itself, then we can have it."

That night a bushel of apples, all the apples on Pastor Fritz's apple tree, was delivered to the boys at Hebron.

Two springs came and went, and both seasons and ever after Gunther's long-cheated eyes were dazzled by the sight of apple trees in blossom.

Two summers, and with them came the event that for the Hebron boys almost equalled Christmas—the annual summer outing to the Obermeier farm in Oldentrup. Two autumns, and school again. By now Gunther was devouring the popular series of children's books about the American Indians written by Karl May.

Two winters. Christmas at House Hebron was even livelier than at Patmos, but perhaps there was a bit more interest there in the gift table than in the crèche.

At Hebron, Gunther's pilgrim soul, which had put to sea at Patmos, sailed steadily onward and outward. Father Mast's morning and evening devotions and Brother Thomas's nightly reading aloud were a constant wind in his sails.

Pastor Kuhlo proved to be as able a proclaimer of God's word to men as he was a trumpeter of men's words to God. And no one—no one in the whole wide world could preach to and reach a boy's secret self as could Pastor Fritz.

In the brain house at the top of the body, Gunther changed from a timid, shy self to a confident, perhaps even proud self—that is, he began to have faith in the idea God must have had when he made him. In the daily mental skirmishes with the other boys—in fun mostly, but sometimes not—he learned that his mind was as good as, if not superior to, the minds of his friends—except Klaus. In Mr. Kunze's school his mind toured the worlds of flamingoes and Eskimoes and felt everywhere at home. In the schoolroom Gunther felt himself supreme—except for Klaus. It is not surprising that Klaus became his best friend.

Gunther's body grew on Hebron farm's milk and eggs, on good Bethel bread made from Bethel-milled whole rye and barley flour, on potatoes, kale, carrots, and cabbage from the Hebron garden. But the muscles to his hands and fingers never forgave their first insult, and he always had to be fed. For the healthy and sound of body who have an unhealthy narrow and biased view of what is pleasant, it is always unpleasant to watch anyone older than three swathed in a big bib and spoon-fed like a baby. But the Bethel eyes, accustomed to seeing bodily blemishes, defects, and weaknesses of every kind, thought nothing of it. The deacon brothers and the Hebron boys dropped food into Gunther's gaping mouth as cheerfully as father robins feed their young.

Since Gunther was included in all the boisterous play, be it up in the Beech Forest or down on the Hebron meadow, his body developed many new skills. In the rough-and-tumble bear-cub wrestling the boys were always doing, he became as quick and expert as any. When the boys wheeled him back to Hebron at supper time, he was as grubby as any of them and got the same good-humored chiding from the Brothers, who had to clean them up for supper. They quarreled and fought, and the other boys soon learned to stay clear of Gunther up on his knees, his arms threshing in all directions. Friendships were made, broken, and mended again. At House Hebron, Gunther became a boy among boys.

It was almost by accident that Gunther learned at last to walk upright like a man. After many attempts and as many failures to balance himself on his unconforming, uncooperative feet, he and his comrades had practically given up the idea of his walking. Perhaps the boys were too willing to push, pull, and tote Gunther around.

At least, teaching Gunther to walk certainly was not their intention when two of them pushed his wheelchair into a flock of geese the others had just teased into a rage—and then abandoned him to the enemy. The boys vanished in all directions. It was just another prank of theirs, and they were just as astonished at the results as Gunther. Deserted by his friends, Gunther cowered before the geese. When the gander arched its snake-like neck and marched with open hissing beak at his bare feet, Gunther did the unbelievable. He bounced from the wheelchair and *ran!* Fully a half dozen or so yards he ran before he stumbled and fell. In an instant the boys were at his side.

"Gunther! You *walked!* You crazy kid, you *walked!*"

Gunther sat up and rubbed his bruised knees. He measured the distance from where he was sitting to his wheelchair.

"I don't remember doing it. But if I did, and I guess I did, then I can and will learn to walk. I *will!*"

"Try it right now," they urged. "Walk back to your chair."

But Gunther's feet refused to remember what they had just done. So then and there a secret conspiracy was hatched. Gunther's feet had proved that they could walk. Gunther's feet would be compelled to walk. They would practice and practice and practice. In secrecy. Up in the Beech Forest. And when they had the annual outing to Obermeier farm in three weeks, Gunther would surprise the living daylights out of Father and Mother Mast, Pastor Kuhlo, and the Brother-deacons. When the horses and wagons drove up to Hebron House to take them on the outing, Gunther would *walk* to the wagon. No wheelchair. No, siree!

In the next three weeks Gunther would have given up time and again, but the combined grit and guts of his friends would not let him. Up on the paths of the forest they contrived the idea of having one of them sit in the wheelchair and Gunther lean his arms on it and push. With the boys running alongside, Gunther reeled and lurched along and somehow learned a crazy way of balancing a body that was all askew. Later he practiced without the support of either chair or friends. The Brothers should have wondered at his bruises when they prepared him for bed at night, but they were quite accustomed to boy bruises and asked no questions. Gunther fell. It hurt. But it was always: "Up again, Gunther! Try it again!"

What Gunther finally achieved may not perhaps be called walking—that is if walking means always to have one foot on the ground. Sometimes Gunther moved with both feet on the ground in a kind of side-sliding motion. Sometimes with both feet off the ground in a kind of hop and skip. And never in a straight line. The worst that could be said was that he walked like an ape. The best, that his walking was a kind of birdlike ballet. But locomotion it was. It got Gunther from one place to another, and his friends were jubilant. After Klaus on a visit to a zoo saw how seals "walked" on land, he called Gunther's way of walking "flippering."

On the day of the summer outing to Obermeier Farm, the boys by agreement clustered around Gunther at the door of New Hebron and waited for the gaily decorated wagons to come to pick them up. When the horses came trotting briskly along, they broke away with a yell and climbed onto the wagons.

"Everybody here?" called Father Mast. Looking back, he saw Gunther sitting in his wheelchair. "You forgot Gunther! Go fetch him, boys."

"Let Gunther fetch himself!" they shouted. That was the cue, and before the astonished eyes of his elders Gunther rose from the chair and flung himself at the wagon. Only with his last foundering step did one crooked foot trip on the other, but he caught himself on the wagon wheel and looked triumphantly up at the grinning faces of his friends.

"Bravo, Gunther! Bravo, bravo, bravo!" Father Mast leaped from the wagon and clasped him to his broad chest.

Pastor Kuhlo promptly blew "Praise God from whom all blessings flow"—and the procession to the country began. Waving their arms and singing at the top of their voices, they rolled through Bielefeld. The more people they saw on the streets, the louder they sang and the more jubilantly they waved. When they came to Oldentrup,. seven miles away, they were still singing.

Father and Mother Obermeier, dressed in their Sunday best, were waiting for them. When they heard the story of the miracle, Father Obermeier clasped Gunther firmly with his stout arm and led the whole Hebron bunch through the stables and stalls to see the horses, cows, and pigs. After coffee and cakes and much laughing at the jokes that flew back and forth between the adults, they played games in the pasture and rode ponies led by the Brother-deacons. After Gunther and Klaus had had their turns on a pony, they went to the stable again and watched the milking. For the first time in his life Gunther heard milk sing against the bottom of a pail and gradually change to a frothy murmur.

When everyone was blissfully tired, they all sat down at tables under the trees to a feast that only Mother Obermeier could prepare. All the juicy homemade sausage that they could eat! Garden peas, picked and shelled that very morning. Bowls of cherries, firm from the orchard. When they were full to bursting, too full to move, their farmer host taught them his favorite hymn by Matthias Claudius, every stanza of it!

> We plough the fields, and scatter
> The good seed on the land,
> But it is fed and watered
> By God's almighty hand;
> He sends the snow in winter,
> The warmth to swell the grain,
> The breezes and the sunshine,
> And soft refreshing rain.

> *Refrain*
> All good gifts around us
> Are sent from heaven above,
> Then thank the Lord,
> O thank the Lord,
> For all his love.

> He only is the Maker
> Of all things near and far;
> He paints the wayside flower,
> He lights the evening star;
> The winds and waves obey him,
> By him the birds are fed;
> Much more to us, his children,
> He gives our daily bread.

> We thank thee then, O Father,
> For all things bright and good,
> The seed-time and the harvest,

Our life, our health, our food;
No gifts have we to offer
For all thy love imparts,
But that which thou desirest,
Our humble, thankful hearts.

Perhaps the most glorious part of their annual summer outing for the Hebron boys was to stay away from their Bethel home until it was dark and the stars came out. They who had to go to bed so punctually, for whom the lights went out at nine o'clock, could stay at Obermeier Farm until the fireflies and the stars came out—until the Chinese lanterns were lit and they could walk once more about the farm with their jovial host and hostess with these beautiful, swaying, colored lights. When they finally climbed on the wagons for the home journey, Mother Obermeier slipped cherries and chocolates into each hand.

"God be with you until next year," called Father and Mother Obermeier as they clattered away.

There was almost no singing on the way back, but when the wagons passed the portal house of Bethel, Pastor Kuhlo stood up and began to blow the Claudius hymn they had just learned.

"Maybe we shouldn't disturb their sleep," suggested Brother Thomas, somewhat timidly.

"Nonsense!" said Pastor Kuhlo. "Everyone at all times of the day and night needs to be reminded to walk humbly with his God and to have a grateful heart. The last stanza, boys!"

So they came home to Bethel singing "Then thank the Lord, O thank the Lord, for all his love."

As they drove past Patmos House, Gunther resolved to visit his old friends the next day and show them that he could walk. Maybe even to Pastor Fritz's house—if he could make it that far. It never entered his head that with over

2000 patients under his care the director of Bethel would not be interested in knowing that one of them had learned to walk. It was as preposterous as to think that for God one sparrow went unnoticed.

TO GLORIFY GOD

After six years at House Hebron Gunther, now 13 years old, could hardly remember when he had not been happy. Not that there were no bleak days there. Or bleakness! Many of the boys had frequent letters and visits from parents and relatives—or went home for birthdays, holidays, and vacations. When Gunther saw these happy reunions or heard his friends counting off the days until "then," he ached because no one ever came to see him and the postman never brought him a letter. His heart ached, too, for his friends on the rare occasions when the misery they kept so deeply hidden bobbed to the surface for one brief moment.

"Why does it have to be me?" sobbed Klaus his first night back at Hebron after a home visit. "It isn't fair! Just because I get these attacks I have to be stuck away in this place the rest of my life. Just because people think it's horrible and ugly to see someone having a fit. They're perfectly willing to watch their own kind of fits—fits of temper and rage and cruelty and violence. But *my* kind of fit they refuse to see. People with *my* kind of fit can't go to their schools, can't get jobs, can't do anything. It isn't fair!"

Gunther reached his hand across the space between their cots. Klaus grabbed it almost savagely.

"And *you*—you don't even have fits! But because you have claws instead of hands and because your feet—."

Suddenly Klaus laughed uproariously, and there was no bitterness in his laugh. "Hey, guys! Here's a riddle for you! Who has a perfect understanding and a perfectly awful understanding at the same time? A good understanding and a bad understanding both together?"

It took several clues from Klaus before the others could figure that one out. In fact, he had to split the syllables and pronounce them very clearly and separately—*under*—*stand*—ing—before they got it. In the process Klaus's black mood scurried back into hiding.

The mostly happy days at Hebron came to an end in 1928. Pastor Fritz announced the plans to move the boys to a new house being built and to move the school to Mamre.

"Hebron has become too small for you lively lads," he said with a twinkle. "You are such human dynamos you are busting out the walls of this place."

It was Gunther who gave the new house a name. When Pastor Fritz asked if they had any suggestion as to what the structure being built farther up the hill should be called, Gunther sang out pertly, "Capernaum."

"Why Capernaum, Gunther?"

Taken somewhat aback by his boldness, Gunther answered modestly, "Well, it's a town on the sea of Galilee that Jesus visited a lot, and once when he was there a

Roman centurion asked him to heal his paralyzed servant, and he did. It's in Matthew, and Luke and John tell the story, too."

Pastor Fritz and Father Mast exchanged smiles. Father Mast nodded slightly.

"Capernaum it shall be," said Pastor Fritz.

In some ways the move to the new house and new school was very dismaying. They had been a close-knit little band, the Hebron schoolboys, and now the old gang was being broken up. There were new faces in Gunther's class at Mamre School and in his Capernaum dormitory room. That in itself would have been all right if—if—.

"They aren't as smart as we are," said Klaus bluntly.

"They do have pretty weak minds, some of them," admitted Gunther.

"Remember the time I complained 'cause people don't like us epileptics around? Well, I have to confess I sort of feel that way about kids that are really dumb. I wonder why we have to be put together with them."

"Yah, I feel that way, too," admitted Gunther, sensing that there was something very wrong about his feeling and that it would make Pastor Fritz sad if he knew that he felt that way.

But the splitting up of one close group was already partly being taken care of by the forming of another. For a year now Gunther had been going to a confirmation class taught by Hermann Wilm, Senior, pastor of the Bethel parish.

In the first place, confirmation was a very special kind of instruction leading to a very special kind of graduation. "Responsible adulthood in Christ," explained Pastor Wilm at their first class. "No longer milk-and-mush babies, but meat-eaters. Men and women able to eat and digest the strong meat of God's word. Strong and able and willing to live the will of God here on earth. Which isn't easy, my friends. Don't fool yourselves. It's not easy to be Christians. Sometimes I have the strong feeling that very soon you sitting in this room will find this out in your own lives. Nor will your two years of confirmation instruction be a snap. God asks a great deal of you. Why should I then ask so little?"

The feeling that they were engaged in something very serious and purposeful was a strong bond among them.

"One more thing," continued Pastor Wilm. "You are going to be examined for confirmation and confirmed together with the boys and girls who do not have the sickness of body and mind that you have. The sons and daughters of our Bethel pastors, doctors, teachers, deacons, houseparents, and workers. Because their physical and mental tools are better, they are being instructed in another class. I am not suggesting that I want you to do better than they. In the Kingdom of God there is not that kind of competition. I want you to prove to everybody that the afflicted in body and mind are not for that reason afflicted in spirit. In fact, again and again I feel that because you are afflicted, God permits you to understand and love his truth even more than those who are not."

"Yes, oh yes!" they all silently agreed. And that was another bond among them.

In the third place, boys and girls went to confirmation instruction together. In Bethel in those years it was about the only place boys and girls did anything together. This proved to be an entirely different kind of a bond.

The female sex is supposed to bring out the best and the worst in males, and Gunther's confirmation class did not prove an exception. Until the boys became used to the presence of girls, there was a bit of showing off.

"O Lord, open the doors of our hearts so that you may enter them," prayed Pastor Wilm at the beginning of their second lesson. After his "Amen" Wolfgang, one of the brightest in the class, waved his hand in the air.

"Yes, Wolfgang?"

"Pastor, my doors are already open."

Smothered giggles on both the girls' side and the boys' side of the room.

"I am happy to hear it, Wolfgang," answered Pastor Wilm quietly. "May our Lord Jesus Christ enter and remain there always."

Somehow Wolfgang did not feel as clever as he had felt before.

It was Klaus who showed off when they were talking about the Israelites wandering in the wilderness and living on manna. Putting on his most innocent face, he asked, "How did God put it there? If he threw it from the sky, it would have been smashed to bits."

Giggles on both sides of the room.

"Ho, ho!" shouted Hans, whose mind was perhaps the dimmest in the class. "It was easy! Everything's easy for God. He let it down gently on a cloud."

"Ho, ho, yourself," snapped Klaus. "The manna would have fallen *through* the cloud."

But Hans refused to be corrected. "Rain falls through clouds, and rain falls gently, doesn't it?"

Gunther, who could not forget that miracles had happened to him, closed the discussion that time. "God lets miracles happen to people, but he doesn't always let people see how they happen."

It was Wolfgang again who grabbed at the chance to tease the girls when the class was reading in Matthew about a man interrupting Jesus when he was teaching and saying, "Your mother and your brothers are outside and want to talk to you," and Jesus answered, "Who is my mother, and who are my brothers?" Ignoring the "brothers" part of the story, Wolfgang snorted, "Served her right! Women are so silly and sentimental!"

"What do you know about it?" From the farthest corner of the girls' side came this fierce cry. Everyone turned to see who had cried out, for everyone heard and plainly understood that this was not just a cry of indignation but a cry of pain. This was not a war cry in the battle of the sexes.

It was Minna. Minna, who was already seventeen and a grown woman. Minna, who had such severe epileptic attacks that it had been thought best not to have her go to confirmation instruction. But she had pleaded for it, and here she was. Minna, whose face was so blemished that for even some of them it was an embarrassment to look directly at it—which was why boys and men especially usually looked past it.

"What do you know about women? About mothers? About mother love? About being separated from a child? About being separated forever and ever from a child? About never being able to have one? Never in this life to hold a baby and know it is yours!"

It was a truth so naked that they looked away from each other, these boys and girls who knew that most of them could never marry and have children, that society would not allow them to have families.

As if that was not enough, Gunther flung another naked truth into their midst. His, too, was a fierce cry of pain. "Wolfgang, if you ever smart off about the Holy Mother like that, I'll—I'll beat you up so you'll never forget it! At least she cared! At least she came to see her son. My mother doesn't ever. Neither does my father. Neither does my grandmother. I don't have a family standing outside wanting to talk to me."

As quickly as his ungainly feet could take him, Gunther left the room. At the door, bitterly conscious of how silly his flippering walk must look, he turned around.

"Look at me, Wolfgang," he said softly. "Take a good long look. I wasn't born this way. I was made this way. You see, I don't happen to have a silly, sentimental mother."

Pastor Wilm buried his head in his hands. The children sat in stunned silence. When he raised his head again, he

94

merely said, "You may go now. You have had enough strong meat for today."

"Is this what growing up means?" Gunther asked himself again and again the autumn before his confirmation, when for a time it seemed as if he had never been happy. Is growing up discovering that you really are not as happy as you thought you were? To have your eyes peeled so that you see yourself and others naked? To find out things about yourself and others that you would rather not know? To discover that you hate? Hate your parents? Hate yourself? Yourself most of all?

For the first time in his seven years at Bethel, Gunther felt lonely. Yet at the same time he seemed to dote on his feeling of loneliness and looked for every chance to be alone.

"You're lucky!" grumbled Klaus, who often had his own black moods. "They let you go walking alone. Me—I always gotta have someone tagging along because I get attacks."

It was not easy to find a place to be alone in Bethel, but Gunther often found the paths of Zion Forest deserted on chill October days. Sometimes he sat on a bench in the outdoor church in the forest, one lonely figure where on great festival days five thousand sat.

One such afternoon he sat with Klaus's words still ringing in his ears. "Gunther, does everyone you meet ask you the same question they ask me—'Klaus, my boy, what are you going to be?' All of a sudden it seems we gotta choose what we're going to do after we're confirmed. It seems that by the day after we're confirmed we're supposed to have a clear call from somewhere. Are the heavens going to open and a voice tell me what I'm supposed to be? Well, I know what I want to be, Gunther. I want to be a pilot. Fly a plane way up there beyond the clouds where the sky is always blue. Can't you just see me tailspinning to earth when I get a fit? No, Klaus will probably be called to shovel manure on one of the Bethel farms. It won't matter if I have a fit and fall in the gutter. Whatever I do, life will be manure."

Unlike Klaus, Gunther did not hanker to find a call from the sky or outside the boundaries of Bethel. Here is where he had found the only security of love he knew, and never in his born days would he forget that. And thanks to Father Bodelschwingh, the founder, there were many open doors to a lifework at Bethel. Gunther ticked them off on his fingers that afternoon, but there was a No at every door.

A deacon like Brother Herman and Brother Thomas— that's what he really wanted to be. If only he could live at Nazareth after his confirmation and become a deacon! He had the mind for it, that's for sure. But there wasn't a chance in the world. A deacon had to be strong enough to lift grown men out of their fouled beds if they had had an attack and in their unconsciousness lost control of their bodies. He had to be able to lift them into bathtubs and scrub them clean. He had to be able to grab fellows much bigger than himself and keep them from hurting themselves in their wild threshing about. He, a deacon? He whose crazy, crooked body went sprawling at the slightest push? Impossible.

If not at Big Nazareth, could he live at Little Nazareth? Be a carpenter apprentice? Learn to run a turning lathe, make bedsteads, chairs, tables? Silly to think of it with hands like his.

Holding his hands up before his face, Gunther counted the occupations they could not do. These crazy crooked hands would not let him be a tailor and live at House Peniel, a shoe___ker at House Horeb, a weaver at Old Ebenezer, a gardener at Sharon. Baker, butcher, candlestick-maker—to whatever occupation Gunther's mind brought up, Gunther's body said No, and his spirit despaired.

The hate buried in his past and the No facing him in his future darkened even Gunther's Christmas that year.

The weekly confirmation lessons seemed to make things worse. His mind easily absorbed the memory work—Luther's Catechism, Small and Big, the Bible verses, the hymns— but more like a computer and less like a thirsty living sponge. For a long time he failed to realize that this was one of the Spirit's ways of working and that the layers of his being were being penetrated all the time. He had still to learn that truths hurt most when they are piercing through those layers and that the real joy does not come until they have gone all the way through.

On the way back to House Capernaum Gunther met Sister Anna of the Patmos House days.

"Gunther! Such a long time! How are you? I hear that you are going to be confirmed this spring. And then what are your plans? What are you going to do?"

"I just received a call to the Scrap Heap," said Gunther coolly.

"You mean you are going to work at the *Brockensamm-lung?* I suppose you will be helping sort all the second-hand gifts that come to Bethel. It's a good work, Gunther, if you do it to the glory of God."

Klaus chuckled at Gunther's black humor and Sister Anna's misunderstanding of it. "To the glory of God!" he snorted. "Better to say to the glory of Grandma Sophie's false teeth, Aunt Alma's old corset, and Uncle Heinrich's discarded eyeglasses!"

Almost as if he knew their most secret thoughts, Pastor Fritz preached about "Calling" that very next Sunday. Gunther and Klaus sat side by side and could not believe their ears.

"In just a few weeks 89 of our young people will stand before this congregation and formally answer an invitation from God. Not an invitation to come to a big party or celebration. Not an invitation to enter some profession, to be a deacon or a bookbinder or a nurse. No, nothing like that. It is a personal invitation from God into fellowship with his Son Jesus Christ our Lord. This invitation does not always make us happy. If we take this invitation no deeper than our feelings, then we are in trouble. For out on the open field of our feelings, the devil, our imaginations, and our Old-Adam nature make us scorn the invitation and urge us to refuse. And if we do not take that invitation any farther than our brains, then we are also in trouble. For the mind can never understand it. Only deep within, where Spirit speaks to spirit, only there can we receive and accept this invitation."

"He didn't have to get so personal," said Klaus on the way back to Capernaum.

"None of your wisecracks, please," said Gunther curtly.

"Confound it, I wasn't!" snapped Klaus.

The boys hardly spoke to each other all week.

It almost seemed to Gunther and Klaus as if there were a conspiracy about getting personal. In his next class Pastor Wilm also picked up that aching subject of what's a guy to do with himself when he's no longer just a boy. "Tell me," he asked, "what do you think is the best work, the truest calling?"

"To be a minister or a missionary," several answered at once.

Pastor Wilm chuckled. "Many people think so, especially ministers and missionaries. But God has different ideas, and I suspect that sweeping streets and mopping floors is just as good and true."

"A soldier," said Wolfgang.

"A mother," said Minna.

"No," answered Pastor Wilm. "You may name all the jobs under the sun, and I will still say No. I believe with Paul and with Martin Luther that the true calling for us human beings is to glorify God, to glorify him in spirit, mind, and body. Whatever we do with our lives, our first and foremost task is to glorify God. On every piece of music Johan Sebastian Bach composed he wrote, 'To God alone the glory.' Tell me now, what do you think of our friend Fränzchen?"

They all thought of Fränzchen, who drove a donkey cart up and down the streets of Bethel and collected garbage and swill for the pigs. Just about all he could say was "Pig swill! Pig swill!" And yet Fränzchen was always happy and cheerful. It made you feel good inside when he passed by.

"Fränzchen glorifies God," came a voice from the back of the room.

"You bet he does!" said Pastor Wilm. "Fränzchen could go around feeling that life has cheated him, that he has an inferior, worthless body and mind, not even good enough for the scrap heap. But Fränzchen's spirit knows that even with his afflicted mind and body he can glorify God. And because he does, he brings joy to everyone he meets. To see Fränzchen makes me love Jesus Christ all the more."

Pastor Kuhlo, too, seemed to be in the conspiracy. The 89 confirmands were to sing a special hymn on confirmation day, and the hymn he chose to teach them was a chorale by Paul Gerhardt, Germany's greatest hymn writer, sung to the music of Johann Sebastian Bach, Germany's greatest musician. What could be more personal than that hymn? "O show thy cross to me.... O make me thine forever.... I joy to call thee mine.... Lord, let me never, never outlive my love for thee."

Gunther and Klaus still pretty much avoided each other until the June-like day in mid-March when the telephone rang in every one of the Bethel houses and everyone was asked to look for Inge. Inge from Patmos had wandered away looking for her beloved Tante Anna. Sister Anna had gone on vacation for two weeks and had carefully explained it to Inge, but Inge's mind could not grasp the word "vacation." To her, Tante Anna was gone and had to be found.

Tante Anna was lost and Inge had to find her. And now everyone in Bethel was looking for little lost Inge.

Gunther and Klaus fearfully circled the ponds in Bethel, not daring to look into the cold murky water. They climbed the hill with scores of others and called into the dark forest that went on and on for miles. "Inge! Inge! Where are you, Inge?"

But there was not even an echo of their own voices. No trace of Inge was found that day or night. For some the search went on all night long. Then, about nine the next morning, the bells in the belfry of Zion Church began to ring wildly. Later it was told that when Pastor Fritz received the message that Inge had been found, he himself climbed the narrow stairs to the belfry and rang the bells. And that the bell rope had swept him off his feet and the bell-ringer proper had to get him safely back on the floor again. Whenever the bell-ringer laughingly told the story afterwards he said, "And I told him 'The cobbler must stick to his last. You stick to your preaching, and I'll stick to my ringing.'"

Everyone who could streamed up the hill to the church from every direction. Pastor Kuhlo stood on the steps playing "Praise God from whom all blessings flow." And there was Inge, wrapped in a warm blanket and safe in Pastor Fritz's arms. He carried her into the pulpit and told them how a woodcutter had found Inge last night about six miles away in the forest. "Tante Anna gone. Inge find Tante Anna," she had said to the woodcutter. Then Pastor Fritz read the parable about the lost sheep in the eighteenth chapter of Matthew. But for Gunther and Klaus, the greatest parable was the glory in Pastor Fritz's face, the sheer joy and love with which he looked at Inge—and Inge laughing and patting his shiny bald head.

"If I ever again talk about being good for nothing, give me a good swift kick in the butt," said Klaus on the way back to Capernaum.

"Same goes for me," said Gunther aloud, but the Gunther deep within sang a freedom song. Not only had his fear of the future vanished, but the icicle of hate had melted. His disgust and his hatred of his parents, his grandmother. His disgust and hatred of his crippled body. He was no longer afraid and sad to be Gunther. There, deep inside, it truly seemed as if he had been born all over again and was brand-new.

So brand-new that on the Sunday the 89 confirmands were examined before an overflowing congregation in Zion Church, there was not a trace of pride in Gunther's mind when he correctly answered every question the other confirmands could not. The old Gunther would have thought, "Listen, everybody. Do you hear? I'm smarter than the preachers' and the professors' and the doctors' kids."

It so happened that toward the end of the long examination Pastor Wilm suddenly decided to ask about the names of all the places in Bethel.

"Wolfgang," said Pastor Wilm. "Can you tell us the origin of the name Bethel?"

"It's—it's a name in the Bible," stuttered Wolfgang.

"Yes, so it is. The names of almost every building in Bethel are from the Bible. But what story in the Bible is connected with the name Bethel? Minna, do you know?"

"Bethlehem, where Jesus was born?"

"No, Minna. Hans-Jürgen, can you answer that question?"

But not even the son of the professor of theology could answer.

"Gunther?"

"Bethel is named after the place where Jacob dreamed about a ladder reaching up to heaven. He called the place Bethel, which means 'the house of God.'"

"And what did Jacob do at that place?"

"He made a vow to God that the Lord God would be his God."

"Just as you young men and women are doing today here in Bethel. Klaus, are there any other buildings in Bethel named after places named in the first book of the Bible?"

Klaus did not know of any others.

"Gunther?"

"Mamre, Hebron, Moriah, and Mahanaim are all names out of the book of Genesis," answered Gunther promptly.

"Tell me, Gunther," asked Pastor Wilm curiously, "how do you happen to know where all the names of the houses in Bethel come from? I don't remember that we studied about that in confirmation."

"Well, you see—" (Gunther flushed and darted a look at Pastor Fritz) "you see, it was I who suggested the name for Capernaum. After that I got so curious about all the other names that I looked them all up in the Bible."

"Boy, did you wow them!" said Klaus later, all admiration and no envy.

"I just happened to get the right questions," said Gunther modestly.

"One question I'll bet you can't answer," said Klaus. "How in the world did the Japanese Christians on the other side of the world know that we are being confirmed and send us these New Testaments edged in gold?"

"Maybe that's what they call 'the fellowship in Christ,'" said Gunther.

It was Gunther's strong sense of the family of God and the fellowship of Christ which made his confirmation day a glorious festival day when it could so easily have been a day of gloom, for it seemed as if everybody else's relatives came except his. The valley between the two low mountain ranges is frequently trapped under rain clouds, but Palm Sunday, March 29, 1929, was beautiful and sunny. When the boys in Capernaum came down for breakfast, they found that during the night the houseparents had decorated the dining room with branches in bud and bouquets of gay tulips, daffodils, and hyacinths. Forever after the fragrance of hyacinths reminded Gunther of this greatest of Sundays in his life—also the ringing of church bells, for Zion's bells rang jubilantly for a full half hour before the service in the church began. Joined by the girls in the class, the boys marched in procession up to Zion church along streets strewn with evergreen branches. Up on the hill in front of House Hermon the two classes met, shook hands, and marched together to the church. Singing their confirmation hymn, "O Sacred Head Now Wounded," they walked down the center aisle.

"Dearly beloved," said Pastor Wilm to them just before their vows, "in Holy Baptism you were received by our Lord Jesus Christ and made members of his holy church. In accordance with our Lord's command, you have been instructed in the word of God and led to the knowledge of his will and of his gracious Gospel, and you now desire to make public confession of your faith and to be confirmed. I therefore ask each of you..."

"Gunther, do you renounce the devil and all his works and all his ways?"

"I do," answered Gunther.

"Do you believe in God the Father Almighty? Do you believe in Jesus Christ his only Son our Lord...? Do you believe in the Holy Ghost...?"

To each question Gunther, the complete Gunther, answered aloud, "I do"—and added fervently but silently, "O make me thine forever!" When Pastor Wilm placed his hand upon his head and read to him the Bible verse that was to be the golden truth for his life, Gunther felt that his prayer was already answered: "Jeremiah 31:3: Yea, I have loved thee with an everlasting love: therefore with lovingkindness have I drawn thee."

Klaus's relatives had come for his confirmation, and Gunther met them all that afternoon at the celebration in Assapheum. But Gunther's family, his family now and forever more, was also there. Father and Mother Mast, Brother Herman, Brother Thomas, the Sisters from Patmos, Leni, Willi. . . .

"Gunther, you my friend," said Willi, squeezing his hand until it hurt.

"No, your brother," said Gunther firmly.

When Pastor Fritz embraced him, laid his cheek against his, and said, "Gunther, *meine Liebling*, my deacon," Gunther knew—and never questioned it again—that in the fellowship of Jesus Christ he, Gunther, had found the dearest human relative a boy could have.

THE UGLIEST OF TIMES

Even though Gunther had grown to understand that a person's chief vocation in life is to glorify God, it was hard to see his friends deciding on their life occupation and not know what he himself was going to do. Whatever occupation his friends chose—whether it was to be metal-craftsmen, woodworkers, gardeners, bookbinders, electricians—it meant that they moved away from House Capernaum to be knitted into a different kind of a family life in a different house. Their old life together as schoolboys had gone forever.

Klaus decided to be an apprentice electrician. "Since I can't ever be a pilot and get myself up there in the air and loop the loop and nose-dive, I'll learn how to put words and music into the air."

"What do you mean—put words and music into the air?"

"Radio-broadcasting. It's the electricians who operate the broadcasting of church services and festivals to the shut-ins in Bethel." How Gunther envied Klaus his specific goal!

Wolfgang chose to be a baker. Klaus said privately to Gunther, "I'll bet it's because Wolfgang is never happier than when his teeth are crunching a fresh-baked crusty roll."

Minna, they learned, had moved to Patmos and was going to help take care of the youngest and most helpless children there.

Klaus, Wolfgang, Minna—in some way each of them would be doing a service that made people's lives happier. But how could he, Gunther, make people's lives happier? No matter how bursting with gratitude to God his heart was, his crippled hands were not worth a straw when it came to doing anything for anybody. Gunther winced with shame when he remembered his bitter remark to Sister Anna, "I have just received a call to the Scrap Heap."

But what about the "Scrap Heap," the *Brockensammlung*, where everybody from everywhere sent everything from old bathtubs and bicycles to old clothes, umbrellas, and razors? In the 39 years of its existence the Collection Center had grown into an enormous service and given work to hundreds of patients.

"Maybe I could pair up the jumble of boots and rubbers and shoes that come in," said Gunther, although not terribly thrilled at the idea of devoting his life to old shoes.

"Then," said Klaus, "you would live at House Tiberias. And what, Smarty-pants, is the origin of the name for House Tiberias?"

As if he were reciting a lesson in a classroom, Gunther answered, "The House Tiberias is named after the place of the feeding of the five thousand at which Jesus said, 'Gather up the fragments left over, that nothing be lost.'"

"Brilliantly answered, my boy! Go to the head of the class!" said Klaus.

But it was to the Christmas House that Gunther finally went to work after talking with his housefather about what he should do.

"The Christmas House is a happy place to work," said the housefather. "Sister Marie and Pastor Fritz's sister, Sister Frieda, are in charge. All year long they fill the shelves with the very best that is sent to Bethel by all our friends, and all year long the housefathers and housemothers come there to select the right Christmas present for each patient in Bethel. In the Christmas House it is Christmas all year long, Gunther."

"Will I live at Tiberias?" asked Gunther.

"Maybe you should live at Heilgarten, with those whose bodies only are handicapped. It's nearby, and you should have no trouble getting to work."

To Heilgarten it was—the rehabilitation center that had been started after World War I to help and to train soldiers or any one else who had lost an arm or leg or both or all of them to live again and work again with artificial limbs. Perhaps behind the decision to send Gunther there was the hope that his limbs, which in their rigidity at least were like the artificial ones made at the workshop in Heilgarten, could be helped to function better.

The move from Capernaum to Heilgarten was not easy. By no means. More than once Gunther, who was supposed to be grown-up now, stood behind the hedge and cried. For one thing, he had no young friends here. The fellows of his own age usually came there to be fitted to artificial limbs and to be trained to use them. They came, stayed but a short while, and went again.

As for the wounded war veterans—it was almost a dozen years now since the war had ended, and the ones who were still there were, of course, the most severely disabled. Not all of these men had found freedom from bitterness in

Bethel. Up until now the grown-ups in Gunther's life at Bethel had been God-praisers. Now he met an occasional God-curser, and his boy-soul, so recently promised to God, shivered. Pastor Kuhlo, who had lost two sons in the war, did not curse God. Father Bodelschwingh, the founder of Bethel, and his wife had lost four children in one month, and they had not cursed God. How many times had he heard Pastor Fritz say that a Christian was not mature until he could praise God even in troubles. Were these bitter veterans Christians? If not, should they be in such a place as Bethel? Yet they were loved and cared for with the same loving care given to utterly, utterly helpless Martin, who was a God-praiser if there ever was one.

It was from Martin that Gunther learned how much is left even when so much is taken away. Martin had lain so long untended in a trench after a shell had exploded near him that gangrene had set in and every limb had had to be cut away. So much that makes a man had been destroyed, and yet Martin's spirit was in no way destroyed.

"Think of it," Gunther told Klaus when he met him on the street one day. "I grouse because I have to ask someone to cut my toenails and fingernails, and Martin doesn't have an inch of arm or leg. But you should hear him play Bach on his mouth organ! The Brothers have fixed his harmonica on a frame in front of him, and he blows away and sounds like a whole orchestra."

It was the suffering Gunther saw at Heilgarten that helped prepare him for the next enormous epileptic attack the world would soon have. For the next war was already in the making. The brains and minds that were to set off this enormous fit that shook the world were already sick and disordered. And this convulsion was going to be so violent and so massive that the world was going to sit holding its head for a long, long time and wonder if it could ever put itself together again.

But it was the work at Christmas House which eventually

moved Gunther into the very heart-center of another war—
one that was even more demonic. It was to be a life-and-
death struggle which threatened him and his friends at
Bethel far more than the bombs which fell on Bethel in
World War II. The seeds of this war, too, were hatched
in the same disordered minds that hatched the seeds of that
other war. Strangely enough, both wars officially began on
the very same day ten years later.

But of course Gunther did not know all this the summer
of 1929. All he knew then was that working with Tante
Frieda and Tante Marie in Christmas House was jolly fun.
He had not realized how much he had missed the motherly
deaconesses with their crisp white caps and big bows under
their chins until he was around them once again.

"What shall I do now, Tante Frieda?"

"Do you mean to say that you have already emptied the
boxes Alfred brought from the post office? Goodness gracious sakes alive, Gunther! I'm going to call you 'Streak of
Lightning.' Here's a box of dolls and teddybears the girls
from Nebo just sent over. Aren't they darling? Don't you
wish you were a little girl and could get this baby doll for
Christmas?"

"Naw," answered Gunther, but he chuckled all the same
and soon found himself singing Christmas carols as he used
his arms and hands like tongs and arranged dolls on shelves.

In August Tante Frieda asked Gunther if he would sing
a hymn for her brother, Pastor Fritz, every morning after
breakfast. "Beginning tomorrow, his fifty-second birthday.
Don't say a word about it. Just stand in the garden right
outside his study window and sing."

"But I'm not a good enough singer to do that," protested
Gunther, astonished at such a request.

"No, you are not Enrico Caruso, Gunther; but there is
more to singing than a wonderful voice."

"Yes, indeed," chimed in Sister Marie. "When you sing
praises to God, Gunther, somehow you remind us that we

are not carrying our sorrows and troubles all alone. Do sing a hymn to Pastor Fritz every day, for he has so many, many burdens to bear."

"What shall I sing?"

"Since it's his birthday tomorrow," said Tante Frieda, "sing a Paul Gerhardt hymn. He loves them so. Do you know 'Evening and morning . . .'?"

> . . . Sunset and dawning, sang Gunther.
> Wealth, peace and gladness,
> Comfort in sadness,
> These are thy works; all the glory be thine!
> Times without number,
> Awake or in slumber,
> Thine eye observes us,
> From danger preserves us,
> Causing thy mercy upon us to shine.

Pastor Fritz and Frau Julia lived at House Burg, which could mean a fortress, stronghold, a place with thick walls, barred windows, heavy doors, and all that. But not with the Bodelschwinghs living in it! With them living there, House Burg was like a house without a roof, without walls, without keys to the doors. Everyone came in and out, and there was hardly any privacy at all. It was a huge stone house built into the hill, the first floor honeycombed with Bethel offices of every kind, meeting rooms, sleeping room for fellow-workers in Bethel. Upstairs was the living quarters of the Bodelschwinghs. Up another stairs was the study in which Pastor Fritz worked and prayed, the study in which his father before him had worked and prayed. Because the house was built into the hill, the three large windows of this third-floor study opened onto a garden and the rising hill on top of which stood Zion Church.

It was to this garden that Gunther came on the morning of August 14, 1929. The casement windows stood open, and he could see Pastor Fritz writing at a tall stand-up desk. Gunther opened his mouth and shut it again. How could he sing to him, interrupt him—the busy director of all Bethel? Silly, silly women at the Christmas House to even suggest it! Gunther turned to slip away, but his feet were not the tiptoeing kind, and he was heard.

"Gunther! My little deacon!" called Pastor Fritz from the window. "Did you want to see me?"

Gunther turned. "Tante Frieda—she—she asked me to sing to you," he stuttered.

"I would like it very much if you did."

The chorale was begun in a trembling voice, but by the time Gunther got to "Order my goings, Direct all my doings," it rang out boldly. By that time, too, Frau Julia was standing beside Pastor Fritz.

"Thank you, Gunther! You have uncomplicated my day," said Pastor Fritz, leaning out of the window and grasping his hand between his two hands.

"Tante Frieda sent you, didn't she?" said Frau Julia. "She's always thinking of nice surprises for her little brother Fritz. Wait a minute, and we'll send a nice surprise to her. Will you help me pick fresh flowers for the house and for Tante Frieda?"

Frau Julia, her gray hair already escaping its pins, was outside in a flash, carrying two baskets and a pair of scissors. She led Gunther through an opening in the hedge to the main garden, which had just as many flowers as vegetables.

"O, goody good!" exclaimed Frau Julia. "The asters look more cheerful this morning. Nothing, Gunther, looks as sad and dismal on a rainy day as a bed of asters. They simply collapse and bend their heads to the ground and get all streaked with dirt. Let's send Tante Frieda a big bunch of purple, pink, and blue asters."

Looking like a bright sailboat in a sea of flowers in her blue homespun dress and lavender apron, Frau Julia skimmed here and there, snipping flowers right and left and filling the two baskets she had hung on Gunther's arms.

"What a sorry world we would be if God had not given us flowers," she exclaimed. Then, as if struck by a thought, she straightened and looked keenly at Gunther. "There is so much talk in the air these days about lives that are not worth preserving. Pastor Fritz gave a great speech against this new evil in the world at Lübeck in January. I must tell him about flowers. Do you suppose the people who are beginning to talk about lives that are not worth preserving feel the same way about flowers? If you could be a flower, Gunther, what would you be?"

Being a boy and not having given much thought to flowers in his fifteen years, Gunther looked about the garden. "That one there," he finally said, pointing to a tall plant with huge flowers of large yellow petals around a big brown center.

"Just like a boy," laughed Frau Julia. "A big, bold sunflower. And so you are, Gunther. You turn to the sun, you look to the sun, you absorb the sun. The look of the sun is painted all over your face. You proclaim the sun wherever you go. That's a good deal more than many theologians can do who have studied God's Word a whole lifetime."

Frau Julia bent to snip a corn flower. "Here's a blue button for your buttonhole, my little theologian."

If anyone was watching Gunther on his way to the Christmas House from House Burg that morning, he would have seen that his normally tipsy walk was tipsier than ever. Gunther himself felt as if he floated to the Christmas House, soaring on the wings of the knowledge that a grown-up had talked to him as if there were no barriers whatsoever between them, none at all. Frau Julia had talked to him as if he were 50 years old—or as if she were 15—or as if he were a visiting important person!

If Gunther's spirit soared church-spire-high on the day he began singing a hymn for Pastor Fritz every day except Sunday, it was cloud-kissing high the day Frau Julia came to the Christmas House and asked if he would like to be her errand boy. At first he could not believe his ears. Frau Julia wanted him as an *errand boy?* He who could not even walk normally—who shuffled and slid and hopped crazily along, zigging and zagging this way and that? "Hop-a-long" some of the kids in Bielefeld had shouted after him one day. When he finally did believe his ears, he knew that he would go to the North Pole and back, walk on hot coals, sharp spikes, anything—there was nothing in the world he would not do if Frau Julia asked him to.

Immediately after he had sung his hymn to Pastor Fritz, Gunther began his daily work as errand boy to Frau Julia. First it was to the bakery to get bread and hard rolls for the day. Sometimes he saw Wolfgang there, swathed in a big white apron, a baker's cap on his head, his dark hair and eyebrows powdered with flour. Gunther greeted him with the good old German greeting that is better than simply saying "Good Day," for it really says "I greet you in God's name."

"Grüsz Gott, Wolfgang!"

"Grüsz Gott, Gunther. How goes it?"

"Couldn't be better!"

Then it was to the store to get what Frau Julia had written on her list of things needed for the day. Then to the post office with her letters, of which she wrote so many. Maybe to the bookstore to fetch a book. Countless times to Old Ebenezer, where scores of Bethel women wove cloth, following the strong, bright, astonishing color patterns designed by Frau Julia herself—for Gunther learned to his amazement that this amazing woman was also an artist. There were messages to Sarepta, the Deaconess Mother House. Errands all over Bethel. From day to day one never knew what, when, or where, for Frau Julia was a helpmate to Pastor Fritz. Both of them knew that Bethel would have lost its soul the day it became just a well-functioning organization. For them no individual ever was a statistical number. If Pastor Fritz or Frau Julia said to a visitor, "We have 2000 epileptics here in Bethel," their hearts did not see the statistics but 2000 Gunthers, Lenis, Willis, Manfreds, Minnas, Klauses, etc. And no day-to-day problem was ever solved by them as a matter of routine. They knew that if ever they did that they would never reach through to the loneliness inside of the person with a need. They knew that whatever other need that person had his most aching need was a deep-down loneliness.

"I guess I'm criticized sometimes for being too spontaneous," Frau Julia told Gunther one day when she was sending him off with lunch for a tramp who had come begging for work and she had given him a garden fork and sent him off to dig new potatoes for dinner. "But when love stops being spontaneous, Gunther, it begins to die little by little."

Frau Julia tucked two rosy apples in the basket. "One for you and one for him." Reaching up to capture her straggling hair, she laughed merrily. "I guess I'm criticized, too, for not paying enough attention to how I look. One day a very proper professor's wife here in Bethel said, 'Why Frau Bodelschwingh, do you know that you have on one gray stocking and one blue stocking?' And sure enough, so I had! So I just said to her, 'Yes, and I have another pair *just like that* at home!' You should have seen her face, Gunther! She looked as if she had swallowed a live goldfish."

A paradox is something that is true but seems to say two opposite things. In his work as messenger boy to Frau Bodelschwingh in the 1930s, Gunther learned what a paradox House Burg was. "Come in without knocking" said the sign on Pastor Fritz's study door, and this was true of the whole big sprawling house of stone back to back with a hill. If it was a fortress, then it certainly was the most get-at-able fortress in the world. And yet at the same time that it stood, so to speak, roofless to heaven and doorless to mankind, it truly was a mighty fortress, a bulwark never failing, against man's most ancient enemy. There are beautiful paradoxes and ugly paradoxes. A great Danish thinker has called Christianity the most beautiful paradox because it proclaims that eternity has broken into time. House Burg in Bethel was a beautiful paradox not only because it was a fortress and yet not a fortress, but because here in this place a man and woman of God held fast to an eternal truth in the ugliest of times.

At first the ugliness seemed to be more of an economic mess, except that this time it was a colossal mess, wider than Germany, as wide as the whole world. In 1929 the economy of the whole world went smash. "The Great Depression" it is called in history books, but this phrase by no means describes the panic and the poverty, the millions of unemployed, the millions of mothers who did not know what to feed their children the next day, the billions of pale, scrawny children.

Beggars and tramps, the great army of the unemployed, came streaming again to Bethel—sometimes as many as 80 in a day. Many of them were sent to Eckardtsheim, the "Bethel on the other side of the mountain," which Father Bodelschwingh had begun a hundred years ago to take care of the unemployed from another war, another fake boom, and another big bust. Here the "knights of the road," as Father Bodelschwingh called them, could eat, sleep, and work again. Here they could live in bright, clean homes with cheerful, loving houseparents.

Instead of climbing the steps to the street door and the Bethel offices, some of the tramps and beggars blundered up another flight of stairs or stumbled to the back door, to the not-so-private quarters of the Bodelschwinghs. And instead of sending them downstairs to the office to go through the routine of being sent to Eckardtsheim, Frau Julia gathered them together as a mother hen gathers her chickens.

"Gunther, please go to the bakery and get some more bread."

"Gunther, please show this young man where he can

wash up and then go to the kitchen and tell Berthe to fix him some tea and sandwiches."

If these men were willing to work, Frau Julia set them to work laying stone walls to shore up the Zion Church hill. It was Gunther who brought them their mid-morning lunch from the Bodelschwingh kitchen. And this was how Gunther became intimate with the economic ugliness of the Great Depression.

Because he lived in Heilgarten until it closed in 1932, and because he came and went daily in House Burg, Gunther also saw the political conflict raise its ugly head in his homeland as if he were watching from a high tower. In Heilgarten he listened to discontented wounded veterans of World War I. When he brought lunch from Frau Julia to the men working on Zion Hill, he listened to the discontented unemployed. In the Bodelschwingh household he could not help overhearing snatches of conversation between leaders of the government and the church.

"What's happening in our country anyway?" Klaus asked Gunther one night in 1932 after a YMCA meeting. Klaus was learning to repair radios now and was hardly ever out of hearing of news broadcasts and political speeches. "Today I heard a man named Hitler almost splitting the tubes with his shouting. Did you hear him, Gunther?"

"I should hope not," said Gunther. "Frau Julia never stands still long enough to listen to the radio. What did he say?"

Imitating the speaker he had heard, Klaus shouted in a harsh, ear-splitting voice, "The streets of our nation are in turmoil! The universities are filled with students rebelling and rioting! Communists are seeking to destroy our country! We need law and order in this land! Yes, without law and order our nation cannot survive!"

"I guess this Hitler fellow is a National Socialist. But who's right, Gunther, the Communists or the National Socialists?"

"I don't really know," confessed Gunther. "One day one bunch of men tells me the Communists are gangsters, hooligans, and cutthroats, and the next day another bunch of men tells me the National Socialists are gangsters, hooligans, and cutthroats. I don't know whom to believe. Shall I ask Frau Julia? She always tells me whatever I want to know."

"I wish I knew!" said Frau Julia when Gunther asked her the next day. Her plump and usually cheerful face suddenly looked worried and sad. "Both parties appeal to people's fears, hates, and frustrations. The Communists collect the bitterly poor who have never had anything. They want a revolutionary society and a new world order. The National Socialists collect the lower-middle class who lost everything after the war. They want everything back that they lost, and they want the quiet, order, and security to enjoy it."

"They both sound all right to me," said Gunther.

"Gunther, beware of cruel and ruthless men with high ideals," said a voice behind them quietly. Pastor Fritz had come unnoticed into the room. "In fact, I would even go so far as to say that we must beware of kind and cultured men with high ideals—if in all their kindness and culture they do not have faith in the Lord God and his Son Jesus Christ, if they do not have his love in their hearts."

On January 30, 1933, Gunther had the flu, and the doctor who was called to Hebron, where Gunther now lived, told him that news had just come over the radio that Adolf Hitler, leader of the National Socialist party, had just been appointed Chancellor of Germany.

A month later Klaus came running to Hebron to tell him that the Communists had burned down the Parliament Building. It actually had been set on fire by the National Socialists and blamed upon the Communists. Enraged at what they thought the Communists had done, the German Parliament swiftly gave Hitler the complete power of a dictator over the German people. *Der Führer* (The Leader) he was called from now on. The Communist Party was outlawed, and the National Socialists became the all-powerful party, the Nazi Party. Party members greeted each other with a stiff raised-arm salute and "Heil Hitler." Their banner was an ancient symbol, the swastika. Brown-shirted militia men appeared on the streets and arrested all "dangerous elements," that is, anyone who opposed the Nazis. Soldiers in black uniforms and shiny black boots were Hitler's private army to enforce his dictatorship and strike fear into anyone who opposed him. In one short year Germany ceased to be a republic and became a military dictatorship.

One morning when Gunther went to the bakery and greeted Wolfgang as usual with "Grüsz Gott," Wolfgang snapped into a stiff salute.

"Heil Hitler!"

Gunther looked at him soberly. "Grüsz Gott, Wolfgang," he said again.

"Heil Hitler!"

"Grüsz Gott," repeated Gunther stubbornly.

"Heil Hitler!"

"Gunther is right," said old Berta, counting rolls into Frau Julia's basket. "Don't be in such a hurry to be a Nazi, Wolfgang. The Party doesn't like us epileptics, cripples, and morons."

"You lie!" shouted Wolfgang.

"Wait and see," said old Berta.

The political ugliness was not as plain to see as the economic ugliness. To Gunther, who came and went in House Burg and overheard snatches of alarming conversation, it was as plain as could be. To Klaus, who listened to another kind of talk and because of his work never missed a Hitler speech on the radio, the political picture looked prettier every day. But Klaus, unlike Wolfgang, was reasonable, and a fellow could argue with him.

"If you won't believe what I say about Germany, just take a look around here in Bethel," said Klaus. "Things are much better here, too. Are there as many beggars and tramps now as there used to be? They say that there are only old men left at Eckardtsheim."

"Sure, but that's because the young men are in compulsory labor camps or training to be soldiers. Pastor Fritz is afraid even our young deacons have to go into military training, and who is going to take care of all the sick in Bethel then?"

"Hitler is giving us Germans back our national pride," said Klaus. "We've been pretty low on the ladder since we lost the last war."

"Sure, sure, we're the greatest! We're the superior race! But if someone's superior, someone else has to be inferior. And who is Hitler saying is inferior, tell me that, Klaus."

"Jews, I guess," answered Klaus in a shamed voice.

"And how do you think we two, you and I, fit into this race of supermen? Can't you just see Klaus the Epileptic and Gunther the Cripple marching—you would march and I, of course, would flipper—straight up to Hitler himself, surrounded by his tall broad shouldered black shirted SS supermen and saying, 'Here we are, Our Leader! Klaus the Epileptic and Gunther the Cripple! Reporting for service, Sir!' "

"Shut up!" said Klaus.

Klaus had nothing to say, either, when Gunther faced him with evidence that Hitler and his Nazi Party were stabbing the church of Christ in the back. Little stabs, at first—and yet not so little. Squeezing Pastor Fritz out of his newly elected office as bishop of the church and placing a Party member in that office was a serious move and attack on the church.

"But in a way I'm glad," said Gunther. "The month of June when Pastor Fritz was gone was awful! Anyway, he's the secret bishop for everyone who calls Jesus Christ his

Lord and not Hitler. Besides, he's got a lot of new problems at Bethel. Do you know that the Nazis won't allow Bethel and other church institutions to ask for help? Remember how confirmands in the congregations near Bethel always collected Easter eggs for everybody in Bethel? Well, this year they weren't allowed to appeal to people for eggs. But one confirmation class just built a big nest in front of the altar, and somehow 2000 Easter eggs found their way into it."

Gunther continued to gather evidence at House Burg for his running argument with Klaus, and Klaus continued to report on Hitler's speeches. But even Klaus began to see the Lie, especially after the 1935 Nurenberg laws against the Jews.

"The guy next to me in the radio repair shop is a Jew," said Klaus glumly, "and he's just as nice as you or I."

On Palm Sunday, 1939, the 10th anniversary of their own confirmation, Klaus and Gunther came to the confirmation services at Zion Church and found its doors smeared with swastikas and the figure of Christ hanging head down on the cross. Five minutes later Klaus had one of the most severe epileptic attacks Gunther had ever seen him have. Gunther and a deaconess sat beside him as he slowly came back to consciousness in the recovery room in the back of the church.

"O Sacred Head, now wounded, with grief and shame weighed down," the congregation was singing.

"I hate them! I hate them!" moaned Klaus.

"No, Klaus, no," whispered Gunther. "Hate is their weapon, not ours."

But that the body of the German nation was building up to a convulsion of demonic violence because of the demonic disorder in the mind of its leaders and that this convulsion would begin in just a few months—this Gunther did not know. His glimpses of the darkness ahead were few and far between and almost promptly erased by his daily joy in being Frau Julia's messenger boy and in seeing his beloved Pastor Fritz. Then, too, something happened in the 1930s that was almost as momentous as his learning to walk. One morning when he reported for work after singing his hymn outside Pastor Fritz's window, he found Frau Julia in more than usual high spirits.

"Oh, there you are! I thought you would never come. Guess what, Gunther! You are going to learn to write. I got the idea this morning when I was in the storeroom and saw Father Bodelschwingh's old typewriter. Those peg-fingers of yours can't grasp a pen or pencil, but they can tap keys. Of course they can. So I carried the typewriter out into that little sideroom, put a new ribbon on it, and there it is waiting for you. If you learn to write on it, Gunther, we will give it to you."

Learn he did—and so quickly that in a matter of months he was typing Frau Julia's letters. And so sure of his words was he that he even dared to guess what she meant when he could not read her hasty writing and she was not there to ask.

Fishing for words now became Gunther's private sport. Up until now words had darted swiftly into his mind like bright tropical fish and as swiftly gone again. Now, with his typewriter, he could catch them in a net and put them on a page. Now he could dip his net into his heart and capture words of love and praise and offer them shyly to those who had loved these words into his heart. Gunther became a poet.

Understandably, Gunther's first gift of words was to Frau Julia and Pastor Fritz. The occasion was their silver wedding anniversary in 1936. April 30, the date of their wedding 25 years ago, was celebrated at Freistadt on the Wietingsmoor near Hannover, where Father Bodelschwingh had established another colony for his knights of the road, as well as for troubled young men in need of guidance.

Even then as well as now, it was just like Fritz and Julia Bodelschwingh to share their celebration with those who had so little to celebrate.

But the next day, the first of May, belonged to Bethel. Six little "angels" in white dresses and wreathed in flowers led the bridal pair to the Forest Church, where all the men, women, and children who could leave their beds were assembled. The bed-bound people heard it all on radio, thanks to Klaus and his crew. Pastor Kuhlo and the trombone band played. The choirs sang. The mouth organ orchestra played. There were speeches, gifts. Frau Julia was moved to tears when the jobless men she had helped in the early thirties presented her with a basket of fruit and read a long poem thanking her for her motherly love.

Gunther's poem was not made public but was shyly presented at the garden gate at dusk when the two tired celebrants came home to House Burg. When they were quite alone in their bedroom, Frau Julia read it aloud. It was a formal little poem, and if it sounded very much like a hymn, that was quite to be expected. Gunther was saturated with them.

> The Lord has been your Leader
> 'Til this great milestone year.
> And you in turn have led us
> To joy from many a tear.
>
> We thank the gracious Savior
> For this loving silver pair.
> For their love, steadfast and true,
> And tender loving care.
>
> Hand in hand together
> March on through joy and woe.
> The Lord Christ is our Leader
> Whatever storms will blow.

Pastor Fritz wiped a mist from his eyes. "If only 'normal' men in the world out there could learn just a little bit from Gunther!" he sighed.

The attack that officially started World War II was launched on September 1, 1939. In a new kind of lightning warfare—*Blitzkrieg* the Nazis called it—powerful armed forces rolled into Poland, supported by planes dropping bombs from the air. The events of that day were to affect millions of lives all over the world. As for Gunther, he felt the effects almost at once—and most painfully. Bethel was immediately ordered to provide beds and nursing care for wounded soldiers from the eastern front.

House Capernaum was one of the houses made over into a military hospital. Gunther was among those evacuated and sent over the mountain to live in the colony at Eckardtsheim, where there now was room because of the decrease in the tramp population. The Bethel spirit of love was just as much there as in Bethel proper, for it was, after all, a Bethel colony. But the long, long year until he could get a room in House Gaza and be a messenger boy for the Bodelschwinghs again was a year of misery.

In a way it was fortunate for Gunther that he had a year's leave of absence from House Burg, for he was spared the agony of seeing his beloved Pastor Fritz becoming engaged in another war. Strangely enough, this war, too, was officially but secretly begun on the same day as the other—September 1, 1939. That was the date found later in a note on Hitler's stationery among his private papers. The note stated simply that Reichsleiter Philipp Bouhler and Dr. Karl Brandt were to be responsible for granting physicians the right to order mercy killing for those whose illness was determined to be incurable.

A simple note, but it was a secret declaration of war. Just who were to be the victims was suggested in innocent green questionnaires that came in October to many sanitoriums and private institutions. The questionnaires were to be filled out by December 1. The names of all patients who could not do productive work, who were mentally ill or insane or senile, who suffered from epilepsy, were paralyzed, or retarded, or who had been patients in an institution for at least five years, or were not of German blood —the names of all such patients were to be listed. According to a new government economy plan, such patients were to be moved to centralized institutions.

So it was a war on the mentally ill, the retarded, the insane, the epileptics, the cripples, the aged. And anyone who had been in an institution more than five years. The Nazi supermen, the physically fittest, had declared war on the weakest, on those they considered unfit to live. And Gunther would certainly be one of their victims, for he was a cripple, could not do productive work, and had been in an institution for sixteen years.

Bethel was not among the first institutions to receive the innocent green questionnaires. But a sister institution did —and filled them out. Why not? It seemed so reasonable— "according to a new government economy plan," . . . "to be moved to centralized institutions." But when the superintendent of that sister institution, Pastor Paul Braune, began to see in newspapers the death notices for the 25 mentally retarded girls who had been taken away from his institution, he became suspicious and turned detective. He quietly collected death notices from newspapers all over Germany and discovered that the patients being moved to "centralized institutions" in a "new government economy plan" were being moved to a place where they were put to death! Between April 10 and May 12 594 such patients had been killed, although the families who received the messages believed that their relatives had died suddenly of pneumonia or flu or some other quick and severe ailment— and that the body had had to be cremated at once. Most of them sadly sent for the urn of ashes and had no suspicions whatsoever.

In the middle of May, Pastor Paul Braune came to see Pastor Fritz Bodelschwingh. The two men sat behind the closed door of the study. When Frau Julia heard Pastor Braune go and noticed that Pastor Fritz did not come out of his study, she began to wonder and climbed the stairs to his study. He was still sitting in Father Bodelschwingh's black leather armchair, his head sunk on his chest, just as Pastor Braune had left him.

"Fritz? My Fritz? Is there anything wrong?" cried Frau Julia, coming swiftly to his side.

"Julia," he said in a voice so dull and dead that it shivered her soul more than if he had cried out in agony, "Julia, what are we men—human beings or wild beasts?"

THE UNSHAKABLE KINGDOM

So now there were two wars raging. In the one war huge Nazi war machines rolled across one little country after another—Poland, Denmark, Norway, Luxemburg, Holland, Belgium, and France. In the air Nazi bombers climbed and dived and dropped bombs that exploded in flashes of orange followed by dirty gray and black as buildings blew up like volcanoes. Then columns of fire, leaping skyward in the night sky. So primed and prepared was the great brutal Nazi war machine that each little country was a pushover. All except England. Protected by a narrow neck of sea from the monster-machines that travel on the ground, England was punished from the air for not being a pushover.

But English bombers struck back. Bethel, lying right next to Bielefeld, a large industrial city, and between a trans-

Germany railway and superhighway, received some off-target bombs. The first bombs fell on Bethel on September 18, 1940. A nurse and twelve patients in Little Bethel, a house for epileptic girls, were killed.

The following Sunday Pastor Fritz preached in Zion Church about "the unshakable Kingdom of God." "If we remain under his rule and in his love, then all things must work together for our good; then even from the deepest grief will grow divine joy. Then we shall be pilgrims walking hand in hand toward the same goal. For God is faithful, by whom we are called into the fellowship of his Son Jesus Christ our Lord."

Across the low mountains in Eckardtsheim some fifteen miles away, Gunther listened to every word of that great sermon on the radio. Wolfgang, who had been sent to work on the farms that had to produce so much more food now that there was war, was sitting in the same room.

"Love, love! Always that mush about love! Why doesn't he say one word about the English murderers! Or about our great Leader?" growled Wolfgang.

"He did," said Gunther quietly.

"Did what?"

"He talked about our great Leader."

"I didn't hear him!"

"Didn't you hear him talk about Jesus Christ, our Lord?"

Of the other war that was raging Pastor Fritz said not one word to the Bethel community. The terror from the skies was already too much for them. He could not add this new and dreadful terror. Yet since the day in May when Pastor Braune laid before him the proof that a war was being waged against the incurably ill and helpless, the two men had been visiting every office in Berlin to try to stop that war. Some of the government leaders were genuinely shocked, for they truly did not know anything about it.

"You must be wrong! This is the kind of sick rumor that gets started in time of war."

"We have proof," said the two pastors, and showed it.

The Party leaders pretended that they knew nothing about it. Even after they saw the proof, they said, "It is a lie, and we have a Gestapo that takes care of people who spread lies." Sure enough, to show that they meant business they arrested Pastor Braune in August and kept him prisoner until October.

Pastor Fritz did not tell any of this to his Bethel community. Neither did he tell them that the green questionnaires demanding a list of the incurables had been received at Bethel in July. On his knees to God in his little room of prayer at House Burg, he prayed that he would do nothing hot-headed or foolhardy that would bring sure death to those who trusted in his care. At the same time he prayed for the boldness and courage to fight against this war upon the weak and helpless, to take all the responsibility upon his own shoulders so that none of his fellow workers could be charged with guilt by the Party and arrested by the Gestapo. He prayed that House Burg, so weak a fortress, indeed, no fortress at all in this new kind of air war, would be a mighty fortress for those the Nazi Party considered to be worthless creatures.

"O Christ Jesus," he prayed, "you who loved the lowliest and the least, help me, guide me, so that not a hair of their heads is touched. Make me as wise as a serpent and as gentle as a dove."

In October Gunther finally persuaded his housefather in Eckardtsheim to let him return to Bethel. But not without some arguing.

"Why, Gunther? It is safer for you here. It is not likely that bombs will fall on our farms. Why should you go back now when more and more are being sent here from Bethel to protect them from air raids?"

"I don't want to be safe. Not when Pastor Fritz and Frau Julia and Pastor Wilm and Pastor Kuhlo and Klaus and all my other friends in Bethel are not."

Gunther was trembling with many mixed emotions when he took his old place in the garden outside Pastor Fritz's study the morning after he settled in his new room at House Gaza. Neither Pastor Fritz nor Frau Julia knew he was back in Bethel. Nor did Gunther know if Pastor Fritz was at home or away on important matters. Nevertheless he decided to sing one of Pastor Fritz's favorite Gerhardt hymns.

"Evening and morning, Sunset and dawning," he began in a voice so weak and trembling that the whole first stanza went unheard.

"Father, O hear me—." The second stanza penetrated the closed windows, and they flew open. First Pastor Fritz's head appeared, and in an instant Frau Julia's.

"Gunther! Gunther! You are back! How good to hear you again! How we have missed you! Come in, come in!"

Inside they hugged him, laughed, and hugged him some more.

"Benita!" Frau Julia called to the beautiful young widowed artist who had studied with Paul Klee at the Bauhaus in Weimar until Hitler pronounced his paintings as no art at all and certainly not German art. Since then Frau Benita Koch had been living with the Bodelschwinghs at Bethel and creating exciting color patterns for the Bethel weavers. "Benita, come see! Gunther is back!"

"Will you be my messenger boy again?" asked Frau Julia.

"Mine, too?" asked Pastor Fritz.

"I have one job for the housefather at Gaza," said Gunther, "and that is to take care of Willi and Otto and get them to the air-raid shelter when the siren blows. Willi is my old friend from Patmos. He is blind, and Otto gets mixed up sometimes and doesn't know where to go. But that is all I have to do, and I would be glad—glad—."

Suddenly, even though he was 26 Gunther was sobbing and crying for joy as if he were six.

In the days that followed, Frau Julia and Pastor Fritz

said nothing to Gunther about the green questionnaires which, if they had been filled out and returned to Berlin, would have sent at least one thousand Bethelers, including Gunther, to their death. (Whatever the Nazis called it— "euthanasia," "a merciful death," "an easy death," "the painless extermination of life that is not entitled to live"— it nevertheless was *death*.) And Gunther was so happy to be back in Bethel that for a while he was completely unaware of the grim battle being waged for his own life and the lives of his friends. It was plain to see that the Bethel patients were nervous and were having more epileptic attacks, but he blamed that on sirens, news broadcasts, and letters from home. Then, too, there was the ugly evidence of war right here in Bethel in the rubble of bombed-out Little Bethel.

"Why are they so nervous?" Gunther finally asked Willi. Willi, who had grown into a quiet, gentle young man, a weaver of mats, could only say what was and never why anything was as it was.

"Everybody scared."

"Why is everybody scared?" Gunther asked Klaus, who was his roommate now and helped him at mealtime and whenever else he needed help. Klaus would not say anything until the two of them were alone up in the Beech Forest.

"The war is going gloriously for us Germans, isn't it? What's everybody so scared about?"

"Sure, the war is going gloriously if you listen only to the German radio. But I've come up here sometimes and listened to the British broadcasts. That's how I heard about Dunkerque and the British saving 300,000 of their troops that our soldiers thought they had trapped. But it's rumors going around that have got some people here in Bethel scared."

"Rumors? About what?" asked Gunther.

Klaus looked around furtively, as if he expected to see

spies hiding behind tree trunks or in the branches. "About people like us being taken away from hospitals and institutions in Germany and killed—and that it's going to start here in Bethel, too, pretty soon."

"Killed!" exclaimed Gunther. "By whom?"

"The Party! The stout and sturdy supermen are out to kill all of us stupid weaklings who get fits and can't hold a gun or work in factories and make guns."

"Cripples like me, too, I suppose."

"Of course! The Party hates you crips just as much as they hate us with fits."

"Pastor Fritz won't let them!" exploded Gunther.

"What's one man against all of them?" said Klaus bitterly.

Only now did Gunther begin to sense the anxiety and tension in House Burg and to understand why Pastor Fritz went to Berlin so often and spent so much more time on his knees in the little room where he prayed. How could he, Gunther, tell him that now he, too, knew about the danger that hung over Bethel—and about Pastor Fritz's lonely struggle against the powers of hate? He decided to try to do it in his daily hymn. The day after Pastor Fritz returned from Berlin and a futile attempt to see Hitler himself, Gunther sang Martin Luther's powerful battle hymn against the powers of evil:

> And though this world, with devils filled,
> Should threaten to undo us;
> We will not fear, for God hath willed
> His truth to triumph through us.

Pastor Fritz opened the window and stood quietly listening to the hymn to its end.

> Let goods and kindred go,
> This mortal life also;
> The body they may kill:
> God's truth abideth still,
> His kingdom is forever.

His tired eyes lit up with a strange burning look that reminded Gunther of the first time he had looked into them, when the love in those eyes had reached into the sea of loneliness in which his Gunther-self was drowning and pulled him out. Today Pastor Fritz's eyes said, "I know that you know, Gunther, but we must not speak about it. Talking will put those we love in even greater danger than they are now." The lips said simply, "Gunther, pray!"

But the rumors continued, for by this time many sad parents and churchmen in Germany knew what Pastor Braune and Pastor Fritz knew—that incurably sick people were being sent to death camps. Rumors that the green questionnaires had come to Bethel also began to circulate. Also rumors that a medical team was going around to all institutions that refused to fill out the questionnaires and was forcibly seizing the records of all patients. It certainly would come to Bethel, too.

"Is my Gertrud safe at Bethel?" wrote a frantic mother.

One day an aged epileptic patient whose head and hands never stopped shaking met Pastor Fritz out on the street. "Are you going to put my name on that death list?"

The houseparents and deaconesses and deacons, of course, heard and overheard these fearful rumors and questions. They came to Pastor Fritz, almost angry in their demands that he make a dramatic protest to the Nazi government. Perhaps do something as Luther had done. Perhaps say, "If you take one of them, you must take me first. Here I stand! I cannot do otherwise."

"If these rumors are true," said one of them, "then you must get up in Zion Church and thunder our defiance of these murderers."

"If I get up in Zion Church and thunder our defiance," said Pastor Fritz quietly, "two things will immediately happen. First, this whole community of poor suffering people will be seized with an appalling convulsion of fear.

Some, indeed, might die of fright. Second, the Gestapo will surely come, and we will lose them all. Dear friends, please believe me. Open opposition is suicide. We must give Hitler no reason to make Bethel a city of death."

Advent in Bethel, 1940, brought the same lift of spirit as in previous years to the very poor in mind who were unaware of the danger that hung over Bethel and themselves. But not to the others. Not to the epileptic men in House Gaza, for many of them were intelligent enough to piece the rumors together and get the ugly picture. Klaus listened to them, but reserved his bitterness for Gunther and the privacy of their room.

"Sure, they know all right. They know what's going on! And they know it won't be long before it comes to Bethel, too. They know we're all trash and that the Nazis are going to get rid of all the trash. Sweep out the litter, the junk, the no-goods. The greatest race on earth is going to be the purest, the most unblemished race on earth. You talk piously about Advent, Gunther. The Nazis are making the Christian Advent obsolete. We're in the Nazi Advent. The Great Coming. Not Christ, but supermen—led by Superman in person, Adolf Hitler!"

"All I can say," said Gunther, miserable before such bitterness, "is that I'm glad Kurt did not live to see this day." But that very day he pleaded with Pastor Fritz to come to House Gaza and lead an Advent Bible study. "There is no Advent spirit there this year."

Pastor Fritz and Frau Julia had supper with the men at House Gaza on the third Sunday in Advent. Frau Julia had brought a huge bundt cake full of dried currants from her own currant bush. She went around the table serving a piece to each man, her motherly face bright with her spontaneous, childlike love. For her, time was now. The past was past, all shiny and forgiven. The future had been given into God's hands. Now was always right now, this unique moment when she could share God's love—and she rejoiced in it. Gunther watched her proudly, felt a glimmer of brightening in the Gaza men's mood. In her presence they truly felt the reality of another world than this dark, suffering world. But the wonderful thing about Frau Julia was that she herself, rooted in another world, did not feel that she was being other-worldly in this world. She just was!

After supper Pastor Fritz read the story from Luke about the birth of John the Baptist, but he talked more about John's father Zechariah than about John.

"God gave Zechariah a *pre*-view of the Coming One, an advance picture of the Christ. You and I have both a hindsight view and a now-view. Tell me! Does Zechariah's preview come up to our now-view?"

The shadows returned to the men's faces, and their eyes shifted uneasily from Pastor Fritz's penetrating gaze.

"Is he a light to us who sit in darkness and in the shadow of death here in Bethel today?" Pastor Fritz leaned toward them, and it almost seemed as if they leaned away from him, away from this question.

"Has the light gone out? Is it all a nice bedtime story?" persisted Pastor Fritz, almost cruelly. "Shall we not celebrate Christmas here in Bethel this year?"

"Pastor, don't talk like that!" cried Willi in a shrill voice.

"You, Willi, my friend," said Pastor Fritz softly, "you who sit in midnight darkness at midday, is this Jesus Christ a horn of salvation, a light in your darkness?"

"Jesus Christ, Son of God, love's pure light! You know that, Pastor. Why do you ask when you know it?" said Willi reproachfully.

"Because we have forgotten! That's why he is asking!" Klaus jumped to his feet. His eyes travelled swiftly around the room. "I don't know about the rest of you, but I know that I for one have forgotten that Jesus Christ is Son of God, love's pure light. I have forgotten that he was born a weak and helpless baby, that he grew up to be the lowest and humblest of men. That he loved the lowest and humblest of people. Useless, no-account people like us. Epileptics like me. Cripples like Gunther. Blind men like Willi. There are some who are saying today that we are not even worth the swill and slops given to the pigs. By loving the likes of us when he was here on earth, Christ showed us that God the Father loves the likes of us. And because he loves us, we ought to love each other. And maybe we ought to love even our enemies. And I don't just mean the English!"

Klaus turned to Pastor Fritz. "Pastor, forgive me for forgetting that Jesus Christ is just as much the light in our darkness today here in Germany, here in Bethel, as he was in Galilee."

"Klaus," said Pastor Fritz humbly, "I, too, forget sometimes. May God forgive us all!"

These days Gunther was choosing with great care the hymn he sang to Pastor Fritz every morning. On the morning of January 6, 1941, he sang the Epiphany hymn:

> How brightly shines the morning star!
> What sudden radiance from afar
> Doth cheer us with its shining?

When he came into the house to get his market basket and Frau Julia's list, Pastor Fritz came down the stairs from the study.

"Good morning, Gunther, bright morning star. On the way to the bakery will you please mail a letter for me?"

Gunther had mailed many important letters for Pastor Fritz, but this one was to Field Marshal Göring, second to Hitler in the Nazi line of command. That this letter was another move in the life-and-death battle for Bethel Gunther was quite sure. Also that Pastor Fritz had not awakened early that morning to thoughts that said, "To arms! To arms! Up and at the enemy!" but to thoughts that said, "Down! Down on your knees! Pray! *This* war cannot be won by deadly, death-dealing weapons or deadly words, but only by the life-bringing weapon of prayer."

The answer to Pastor Fritz's letter of January 6 was not written until January 29, and not by Field Marshal Göring but by one of his underlings. Gunther, of course, did not know what was in that letter until long after Germany's defeat the spring of 1945 and Pastor Bodelschwingh's death in January, 1946. When the two letters finally were made public, Gunther could not help comparing the coolness, curtness, and shortness of the answer to the earnestness and length of the letter he had posted for Pastor Fritz. The answer read:

> Dear Mr. Von Bodelschwingh:
>
> The Field Marshal has personally read your letter of January 6. Our inquiries have led us to conclude that your statements are somewhat inaccurate, for the most part wrong.
>
> The Field Marshal has asked Dr. Brandt of Berlin to provide you with the necessary information. Dr. Brandt will get in contact with you personally.
>
> Heil Hitler!
> BODENSCHATZ

Ungracious though it was, the letter provided Pastor Fritz with a name. Dr. Brandt. Maybe he was the key man. Again Pastor Fritz was off to Berlin. When he returned, Gunther was typing a letter for Frau Julia, and he could not help overhearing what Pastor Fritz said to his wife.

"There is hope, Julia, there is hope! Dr. Brandt is Hitler's personal physician and has some influence with him, I think. He promised to come to Bethel to talk. I can't talk with him there in Berlin surrounded by uniforms,

137

clicking boots, Heil Hitlers, and all that. He also promised that nothing would happen in Bethel before he comes."

Hardly ever bitterly cold, winter in northern Germany can be dismally and damply cold. But in February come strong hints of spring. A greener green in the permanent stain on the trunks of the beech trees. Swelling buds. Tulips and crocuses and daffodils poking out of the ground. Spring is nowhere as welcome as in the Bethel valley, for the childlike mind adores the future that spring spells. Only adult minds are tired of the future before it ever comes. But all joy in the signs of spring was blotted out this year by the fear that many would not live to see another spring. Fear hung like a thick fog over Bethel.

"The Medical Murder Commission is coming any day," said Klaus in the middle of February. "I feel it in my bones."

"I talked to my bones this afternoon, and they didn't tell *me* that," said Gunther, trying to make a joke of it.

"Sorry, Gunther, your bones are as stubborn and unfeeling as cobblestones," said Klaus unkindly.

Gunther flushed angrily and felt like telling Klaus that he, Gunther, had it on sound authority that nothing would happen at Bethel until Dr. Brandt, Hitler's private physician, had come to talk personally with Pastor Fritz. But loyal messengers were not blabbermouths. Not even with his best friend would he share any information he heard or overheard at House Burg. Not now, anyway. Not until everything was in the open.

When Gunther came to the garden outside Pastor Fritz's study on the morning of February 19, he could see that the pastor was not there. "Has he gone to Berlin again?" he wondered, and went in to greet Frau Julia and ask her what he should do today. But Frau Julia was not there. None of the big family that lived and ate under the Bodelschwingh roof was there. From the looks of the table everyone had left in a hurry. Halves of buttered hard rolls still on the plates. Napkins not tucked back into napkin rings. Chairs not pushed back into place. Gunther felt a clutch of fear in his throat. Had the Gestapo come and arrested Pastor Fritz? Perhaps someone in the Bethel offices below could tell him.

Gunther met them all coming up the stairs. Pastor Fritz, ashen and trembling, brushed past without a word and went on up the stairway to his study. Behind him came Frau Julia, Pastor Fritz's sister Frieda, and the others, their faces crumpled into anxiety and grief.

"Gunther, they've come!" said Frau Julia.

Gunther did not have to ask *who* had come.

"Eighteen doctors and eighteen secretaries. They brought their own typewriters," said Pastor Fritz's secretary, still in a state of shock, for they had burst in without knocking just a half hour ago.

"He promised! He promised!" cried Pastor Fritz, who had come out of the study again and stood at the top of the stairs.

"Fritz! Fritz!" sighed Sister Frieda, "I don't know whom you mean, but all your life you have trusted people too much!"

"I'm going to write him a letter right now. You can take it to the post office, Gunther. Or shall I go to Berlin and see him face to face? Julia, what shall I do? Ah, what is the use of doing anything! Of what use have been all my letters—all my visits to Berlin! All is lost now. They are all lost—all my Patmos children. All my Bethel children who will not be able to answer their questions sensibly. Lost! Lost!"

Pastor Fritz went back into the study and closed the door. Frau Julia and Sister Frieda looked at each other, their anxiety now for the crushed and broken husband and brother. Sister Frieda's face was the first to uncrumple.

"Gunther," she said, "go out in the garden and sing to him as you always do."

Through the windows facing the garden, Gunther could see Pastor Fritz sitting at his father's desk, his head buried on his arms. Never had he looked so heartsick, so defeated. Gunther knew that if he did not start singing at once, he, Gunther, would burst into the wildest weeping, and that he must not. Frau Julia and Sister Frieda had not asked him to come out here in the garden to cry. "Put thou thy trust in God," he began, very slowly, giving each syllable of each word its fullest sound, chanting the words so earnestly that he faulted the music. It was the *message* that somehow had to get through to that despair.

Before Gunther had finished two lines of the first hymn, Pastor Fritz rose and came to the window. The way he looked out at him was so strange that Gunther's voice faltered and stopped. It was as if a total stranger were looking at him for the first time and sizing him up. All of a sudden Gunther felt the ugliness of his deformed body, the ugliness of his gravelly voice that was almost as deformed as his body. All of a sudden his standing here in this garden and singing a hymn to this man seemed utterly, utterly ridiculous. Tears scalded his eyes.

"Uncle Pastor!" he cried, reverting to the old Patmos name. "Why do you look at me like that?"

"I looked at you as they, the medical examiners, will look at you. I was listening to you as they will listen to you. I was trying to see and hear you as they will see and hear you, for I am afraid that they have neither eyes nor ears to see or hear you. Forgive me, Gunther. Now sing to me, please. And pray for me. Pray without ceasing for me today, for it is the darkest day in my life, the darkest day in Bethel's history."

In the reflection of the self he now saw in Pastor Fritz's eyes, Gunther sang a hymn by Paul Gerhardt. Pastor Fritz sat in the big leather chair and listened, his head bowed on his hands.

Put thou thy trust in God,
In duty's path go on;
Walk in his strength with faith and hope,
So shall thy work be done.

Commit thou all thy griefs
And ways into his hands,
To his sure truth and tender care
Who earth and heaven commands.

Who points the clouds their course,
Whom winds and seas obey,
He shall direct thy wandering feet,
He shall prepare thy way.

On the way to the bakery ("Life must go on," Frau Julia had said), Gunther met Otto.

"Please pray for Pastor Fritz today."

"Why today?" asked Otto. "Is he sick?"

"No, he is fighting a great evil that will hurt all of us here at Bethel. Today he must win, or the battle is lost."

"I will pray," said Otto soberly.

"Guess what!" said Klaus as he spooned lentil soup into Gunther's mouth at the noon meal in Gaza. "I have the honor of being the first man in Gaza to meet the medical examiners. At one o'clock sharp in Hebron."

Gunther choked and coughed. Klaus calmly wiped the sprayed soup from his own and Gunther's face and shirt. "Cool it, Gunther! You'll need all your good sense when your own time comes."

"It's *you* I'm worried about, Klaus. Promise that you won't be rebellious and reckless! Don't say anything that will make them put you on the—."

"On the death list? Don't worry, Gunther. I have it all planned out. I'll march in briskly, holding my right arm out stiff and high, and when they all do the same and say

'Heil Hitler!' I'll say, 'The snow is *that* high down in Berchtesgaden this winter!''

"Klaus, no, you wouldn't!"

"I just might!"

"Klaus!"

"Shut up and eat your soup like a good little boy."

When he returned to House Burg after dinner, Gunther found it in a new and quite different flurry of excitement. Frau Julia was quite unable to collect her thoughts and think of errands for him.

"Dr. Brandt is here! He came right after dinner, all unannounced. And he didn't know anything about the Medical Commission's being here. You should have seen his face when he found out! So he really didn't break his promise. They are up in the study talking right now. Oh, Gunther, everything depends on this talk. Everything! I think the most important work you can do is to go to your room and quietly pray. At four you can go to the greenhouse and get two dozen daffodils to remind us of spring, that there *is* a spring."

Before returning to House Gaza, Gunther went up the hill to Zion Church to pray. When he walked through the Forest Church an hour later, he met Pastor Kuhlo sprinting along, his black cape blowing in the breeze. There was not the slightest evidence that in three short months this amazingly energetic "General of the Brass Choirs" would be dead.

"Gunther, my boy, we meet just about where we met for the first time years ago. How old are you now? Twenty?"

"Twenty-seven, Pastor."

"Twenty-seven! I see I will have to transpose you in my mind from the key of boy to the key of man." Pastor Kuhlo chuckled, but after a long, penetrating look at Gunther he suddenly sobered. "When I see you and your friend Klaus together in church on Sunday, I think of two keen-eyed eagles. Today I must say you look like a doleful rook. What is it, Gunther?"

"Everything is wrong, Pastor! Everything! Pastor Fritz is facing Dr. Brandt from Berlin, and Klaus is facing the Medical Commission."

"Maybe I should go down to House Burg and play this good fighting hymn," said Pastor Kuhlo, putting his trumpet to his lips.

> Rise, ye children of salvation,
> All who cleave to Christ the Head,
> Wake, awake, O mighty nation,
> Ere the foe on Zion tread;
> He draws nigh, and would defy
> All the hosts of God most high.

When the last notes died from Zion Hill, Gunther said quietly, "It's a wonderfully proper hymn, Pastor Kuhlo. The foe is really treading on Zion Hill. But I think maybe this is not the time to go to House Burg to play it."

When Gunther got back to his room at Gaza he found Klaus lying on his bed, his eyes closed.

"Klaus, are you sleeping?" whispered Gunther.

"No, I'm dead."

"Please, Klaus!"

"No kidding. I'm as good as dead."

"O, Klaus, were you reckless and rebellious? Did you make them angry?"

Klaus opened his eyes and burst out laughing. "Come to think of it, Gunther, that was a smashing answer I gave them! Only a genius could think of it. Do you realize that you are living with a genius?"

"Klaus," said Gunther frantically. "What did you say?"

"They asked me what I thought of our Leader, and I promptly threw a fit. O, it was real all right, Gunther. And from what Brother Rolf, who brought me back here, says, it was a beaut! I crashed to the floor, screamed like a peacock, threshed around like a chicken with its head cut off, foamed at the mouth. The pretty secretary ready to type my answer ran out of the room. Wouldn't you say that was an appropriate answer to such a question?"

Klaus turned his face to the wall. "Well, goodnight, Gunther. Wake me up when the bus comes to take us whose life is not worth preserving to the Death Camp."

Gunther sagged onto his own bed, feeling as if his whole world was having an epileptic seizure, as if nobody was in control, nobody was steering. He lay back on his pillow, closed his eyes wearily. Let the world smash up! It would be so nice to have it all over! Total blackout. Forever and ever. No coming back to consciousness. No hangovers.

So life-weary was Gunther for a brief spell of time that when he did finally open his eyes everything was blurred. The objects in the room flickered dimly in and out of his mind. The canary cage blinked in and out—the silent canary a bleary, tarnished yellow. One object, however, floated into his mind, floated out, floated in again and stayed there as though suspended in the air before him. It was his confirmation Bible verse, illuminated by one of the Bethel artists, framed by a Bethel craftsman, and hanging on the wall alongside his bed:

> Yea, I have loved thee with an everlasting love;
> therefore with lovingkindness have I drawn thee.

The words seemed to float from the frame and hang buoyantly before his eyes, glowing with a halo of light that was not the artist's gilding. Gunther stared in wonder, his mind wide-awake now, as clear as air. Had that everlasting love ever gone back on him, Gunther? No, of course not! Would an everlasting love like that *ever* give up and let go? No, never! Sure the world of men was in convulsion, *but it would not fall apart!* The God of everlasting love would save men from this fit of hate, too. How could he ever have doubted it!

When the light faded and the words were back in their frame on the wall and they and everything else in the room quite normal again, Gunther turned on his side toward Klaus.

"Klaus?"

"Has the bus come already?"

"No bus is coming."

Klaus turned and faced Gunther.

"Who says?"

"Pastor Fritz is talking with the key man in this whole terrible affair right this very minute. Dr. Brandt. He is Hitler's own doctor, and—."

"You mean it was Dr. Brandt who sent this medical team here today to make out the death list?"

"No, he didn't know anything about their coming to Bethel today."

"Then I'd say he's a pretty poor key and doesn't fit the lock."

"But he *is* a key person! Not long ago I mailed a letter from Pastor Fritz to Field Marshal Göring, and I'll bet Göring sent Dr. Brandt to Bethel today to talk over the whole matter of mercy-killing."

"Don't give it that sweet-smelling name, please. Call a rotten egg a rose—it still smells bad. Call it what it is— murder."

"Pastor Fritz will win him over to his side. It will be a terrible struggle of words. Not loud and angry, but quiet and strong—like Pastor Fritz. Pastor Fritz's words will struggle with Dr. Brandt's words. In the end Pastor Fritz's words will win."

Klaus sat up and swung his feet off the bed. He leaned toward Gunther. His dark eyes flashed. "A beautiful picture! You're a real poet, Gunther. I, however, am not. I can't see it. What can Pastor Fritz possibly say to a fanatic

Nazi to change his mind? Hitler thinks he's going to win this war. Even if Germany lies in smoking ruins all around him, he'll still think he's going to win the war. Fanatics can't be convinced."

"Maybe Dr. Brandt isn't a fanatic Nazi! Maybe he's a reasonable man. Maybe he's a gentleman of the old school, as they say. Pastor Fritz will show him all the evidence about people from other institutions being taken away and killed."

"Don't be stupid! What good will all the evidence in the world do? Dr. Brandt believes in rubbing out the incurables and the idiots. He's a scientifically trained man, and by all his scientific principles the human race is better off rid of us."

"Go ahead, Klaus—."

"What do you mean—go ahead, Klaus?"

"If you think you know what Dr. Brandt will say, well, then go ahead and say it. I'm curious to hear your reasoning. But don't be sarcastic and bitter, for I don't think Dr. Brandt would talk like that to Pastor Fritz."

Klaus's voice was suddenly harsh. "We're not kids any more, you and I! We're past make-believing and playing war games with our wits. Least of all to make games out of dying. *Our* dying, Gunther, you the Crip and I the guy who throws fits."

Now it was Gunther who swung his feet off the bed and faced Klaus, eyes flashing.

"I'm not proposing fun and games, Klaus. I'm proposing a wrestling match between—between—well, between a mind like Pastor Fritz's, full of Christ's love, and a mind like Doctor Brandt's, full of smart and sensible-sounding reasons. And you're absolutely right! It *is* a life-and-death struggle. And it's not just about you and me, or just about all of us in Bethel. This dialog is going to go on and on all over the world and as long as there are human beings."

"I get it! I get it!" Klaus jumped up in his excitement.

"With something so important going on, you and I have got to get into the act!"

"I've prayed about it. I was on my knees a whole hour up in Zion Church. Now I want to *think* it. I want to try to think what I think Pastor Fritz is saying to Dr. Brandt."

"And I'll answer the way I think Dr. Brandt would answer. Lord knows, I've heard plenty of their phony philosophy on the radio! Well, here goes!

"My dear Pastor von Bodelschwingh!" Klaus's voice became polite and smooth. "I understand your concern for your people here in Bethel. But you must try to understand that the Fatherland only intends to eliminate the very worst cases, those who are completely worthless to society, those who not only are not able to contribute anything to the economy but are a fearful drain on the nation. They take up beds needed for our wounded soldiers. They eat food that the normal and productive people desperately need. In fact, I am told that epileptics have ravenous appetites. After they have had a fit their alimentary canals gurgle and burble and hiss for food. They roar for food. Those epileptic unfits are taking the food out of the mouths of the fit."

"Now you're being Klaus and not Dr. Brandt!" interrupted Gunther.

"So I am. Sorry. —In short, my dear Pastor von Bodelschwingh, we find that it is a scandalous waste of food and space and money and manpower to care for completely useless people. It is these people, and only these people, the standard our top medical experts have established will eliminate."

Gunther bowed his head on his arms for a moment and then raised his eyes to Klaus. "You speak of a standard for eliminating the unfit, Dr. Brandt. Are you speaking of broken-down machines that cannot be repaired—or of human beings? If you are speaking of human beings, then your standard is inhuman. It is also inhuman to speak of helping some humans by murdering other humans. Where do you get the right to be inhuman in order to help some humans?"

"If you want to talk about being human, then may I ask if there is anything human about these people? Is there any human value in living for some of these poor creatures that are born without a glimmer of intelligence? Or born monstrosities, freaks of nature? Does life mean anything to them compared to the life we experience? Is there any pleasure for them in being alive? Aren't they better off dead?"

"Your questions need to be answered one by one. First of all, may I say that these children are just as much God's children as you and I."

"Really, now, your God has some rather startling off-spring!"

Gunther drew in his breath sharply, let it out slowly. "If Dr. Brandt would really say something as blasphemous as that, I think Pastor Fritz would ignore it. His father once told him never to argue with unbelievers and blasphemers but just speak simply of his own faith."

"O.K.! Ignore it, then. I think it's your move, Pastor von Bodelschwingh!"

"According to you, Dr. Brandt, there are people who are non-human. Your standard is supposed to separate humans from non-humans, and the non-humans are to die. Would you call that a human standard?"

"Yes, for I do not call the lives these poor creatures live human."

"Where is the dividing line? When does a human life become non-human?"

"When it cannot respond to another human being in a human way. When it is not able to have human association with anybody."

"Dr. Brandt!" Gunther's voice rang with triumph. "That cannot be said of even the weakest in mind and body here in Bethel. I must say that I have never in my life met such a person, and I have spent my whole life here in Bethel. If you were to say that of anyone here in Bethel, I'm afraid I would have to ask *you*, Dr. Brandt, if *you* are capable of human association with another human."

"Bravo, Gunther! Bravo!"

"You are forgetting yourself, Dr. Brandt," said Gunther dryly. "Then I think Pastor Fritz would talk about his Patmos children. He would tell Dr. Brandt some of his wonderful experiences of miracle-responses to love . . ."

"Like yours."

"Like mine. And then I think he would . . ."

"You are forgetting yourself, Pastor von Bodelschwingh."

"Therefore, Dr. Brandt, no rulers on earth can make a standard that decides what is human, what human life is worth preserving, what human life is not worth preserving. God alone can give us that standard. And he has done so, Dr. Brandt. The answer to the question about the worth of human life is Jesus Christ. First of all he became human. And in his life here on earth, whom did Jesus Christ place first in his love and concern? Tell me that, Dr. Brandt!"

"I prefer to remain silent before that question, Pastor von Bodelschwingh."

"Dr. Brandt, before the answer to that question all of us have to be silent. The poor, the wretched, the helpless, the lonely, the sick, the crippled, the epileptics—that was Christ's standard here on earth. It is his standard today. It is the standard we live by here in Bethel. We can allow no other standard than God's here, for here in Bethel God rules!"

"Like King Agrippa, I must say, 'Almost you persuade me to believe,' " said Klaus, and there was sheer admiration in his eyes. "I couldn't have done better myself in the role of Pastor Fritz," he added slyly. "But then you had a better case, and I didn't believe in my case at all. Besides, you see and hear Pastor Bodelschwingh every day, and I've never seen Dr. Brandt in my life and never want to. Besides—."

"In short, you admit you lost!" laughed Gunther.

"No," Klaus said, "I didn't lose. I gained—my life."

At 4:30 Gunther came back to House Burg with his arms full of yellow daffodils. Frau Julia was Frau Julia again, and she received both him and the daffodils with open arms.

"Now we no longer need the daffodils to lift our mood, Gunther. Now they *describe* our mood. Now they celebrate our mood. Get me the pewter pitcher and the pottery bowl, please, and I'll fix a bouquet for the living room and one for the dining room."

As her hands deftly arranged the flowers, Frau Julia jubilated on and on. "Such a long talk it was! Three hours without stopping! I served them tea after the first hour, and they were talking back and forth. But when I came to get the teacart an hour later, Dr. Brandt was mostly silent. And Pastor Fritz—O, Gunther, you should have heard him! I do believe that icy mountains would melt if Pastor Fritz talked to them like that! And do you know, Gunther, that Otto came and stood out in the garden when I was backing out the door with the teacart? And that he stood there silently all the last hour they talked? After Dr. Brandt left, Pastor Fritz went out to him and asked, 'Did you want anything of me, Otto?' And Otto said, 'No, Pastor, I just wanted you to know that we are all behind you today.' Do you know what Pastor Fritz said to me? 'With Gunther singing hymns in the morning and Otto standing watch and everybody praying, how could we lose the battle!' There, do you think they look nice? This pottery bowl of daffodils is for the living room. Pastor Fritz is in there resting until supper, but he always loves to see you. Will you dance the daffodils in to him, please?"

"Me—dance?" Frau Julia was amazing, but this was almost too amazing.

"Gunther," she said, giving his shoulder a loving pat. "To me you move like a ballet dancer."

Gunther hoped to place the bowl of daffodils on the center table quietly and slip away unnoticed, but Pastor Fritz opened his eyes. His smile erased the tired sagging lines on his face.

"I'm glad to see you, Gunther. I want to thank you for singing that particular hymn especially today. You see, Gunther, today I fought the hardest battle in my life."

When Gunther closed the door on House Burg on his way home to Gaza, he stopped and looked up at the sky. Would the English bombers come tonight? How helpless against them this "fortress" house was! And yet in this other war between two philosophies of man, between a Christian and a pagan view of man, what a fortress it was for Bethel and for all Germany! What a fortress for the whole world!

EPILOG

Thirty-four years have passed since that day when Pastor Fritz von Bodelschwingh fought and won the hardest battle of his life—the battle to save the patients with severe physical and mental handicaps from being put to death by a government that did not think their lives worth living. The world war Hitler started ended for the Germans in the spring of 1945. On April 1, 1946, Pastor Fritz von Bodelschwingh died.

Dr. Karl Brandt, Hitler's personal physician, who had been placed in charge of the euthanasia program, was tried in the Nuremberg trials, was convicted, and put to death. In his response to the verdict, Dr. Brandt expressed the wish that Pastor Fritz von Bodelschwingh were still alive, for he could and would tell them all that he, Dr. Brandt, was not the monster his accusers had made him out to be.

The war upon the severely handicapped in body and

mind did not end with the defeat of Nazi Germany, the death of Hitler, and the trial and execution of Dr. Brandt. It still goes on in the world, and it will go on as long as there are people who do not know what it is to be human, as long as there are people who think some lives are not worth being allowed to live. Or not worth being born! As long as there are people who think this way, there will be a battle between them and those who believe that euthanasia and abortion are murder.

Bethel is still a valley of the sick. In 1972 there were 6311 patients—among them mentally ill, mentally retarded, mentally disturbed, and alcoholics as well as epileptics.

Bethel is still a valley of healing and uses the healing Word of God, the healing Spirit, and healing love as much as ever it did. It also uses the most modern methods of research into the causes and cures of the illnesses that bring patients from all over the world to this valley. It is one of the world centers for the study of epilepsy.

Bethel is still a valley of love, of work, of art, of music. Long before people began talking and writing about the therapy of love, of work, art, and music, Bethel patients were making music, creating art, doing meaningful work, loving and being loved. Pastor Johannes Kuhlo is long since dead, but every festival occasion in Bethel is still celebrated by choirs of voices, brass, and mouth organs. And anyone and everyone who is buried in the hilltop cemetery at Bethel is trumpeted to his final resting place.

Gunther is 62 years old now and is still pecking out poems for Bethel's many festivals on his typewriter. He still "flippers" up and down the up-and-down streets of the valley. He has other and new friends, for those who first gave him the gift of love are dead and gone from Bethel. Until that day when he, too, goes to join those blessed ones who gave him his first taste and glimpse of the heavenly home, Gunther will go on living happily in Bethel.